S. HRG. 113–153

SECURITY AND GOVERNANCE IN SOMALIA: CONSOLIDATING GAINS, CONFRONTING CHALLENGES, AND CHARTING THE PATH FORWARD

HEARING

BEFORE THE

SUBCOMMITTEE ON AFRICAN AFFAIRS

OF THE

COMMITTEE ON FOREIGN RELATIONS UNITED STATES SENATE

ONE HUNDRED THIRTEENTH CONGRESS

FIRST SESSION

OCTOBER 8, 2013

Printed for the use of the Committee on Foreign Relations

Available via the World Wide Web: http://www.gpo.gov/fdsys/

U.S. GOVERNMENT PRINTING OFFICE

86–352 PDF   WASHINGTON : 2014

For sale by the Superintendent of Documents, U.S. Government Printing Office
Internet: bookstore.gpo.gov   Phone: toll free (866) 512–1800; DC area (202) 512–1800
Fax: (202) 512–2104   Mail: Stop IDCC, Washington, DC 20402–0001

COMMITTEE ON FOREIGN RELATIONS

ROBERT MENENDEZ, New Jersey, *Chairman*

BARBARA BOXER, California	BOB CORKER, Tennessee
BENJAMIN L. CARDIN, Maryland	JAMES E. RISCH, Idaho
JEANNE SHAHEEN, New Hampshire	MARCO RUBIO, Florida
CHRISTOPHER A. COONS, Delaware	RON JOHNSON, Wisconsin
RICHARD J. DURBIN, Illinois	JEFF FLAKE, Arizona
TOM UDALL, New Mexico	JOHN McCAIN, Arizona
CHRISTOPHER MURPHY, Connecticut	JOHN BARRASSO, Wyoming
TIM KAINE, Virginia	RAND PAUL, Kentucky
EDWARD J. MARKEY, Massachusetts	

DANIEL E. O'BRIEN, *Staff Director*
LESTER E. MUNSON III, *Republican Staff Director*

————————

SUBCOMMITTEE ON AFRICAN AFFAIRS

CHRISTOPHER A. COONS, Delaware, *Chairman*

RICHARD J. DURBIN, Illinois	JEFF FLAKE, Arizona
BENJAMIN L. CARDIN, Maryland	JOHN McCAIN, Arizona
JEANNE SHAHEEN, New Hampshire	JOHN BARRASSO, Wyoming
TOM UDALL, New Mexico	RAND PAUL, Kentucky

(II)

CONTENTS

Page

Aynte, Abdi, director, Heritage Institute for Policy Studies, Mogadishu, Somalia..34
    Prepared statement 37
Coons, Hon. Christopher A., U.S. Senator from Delaware, opening statement .   1
Dory, Amanda, Deputy Assistant Secretary for African Affairs, U.S. Department of Defense, Washington, DC..8
    Prepared statement 10
Flake, Hon. Jeff, U.S. Senator from Arizona, opening statement................................3
Hogendoorn, Dr. E.J., deputy director for Africa, International Crisis Group, Washington, DC 40
    Prepared statement 43
Le Sage, Dr. Andre, senior research fellow for Africa, Institute for National Strategy Studies, National Defense University, Washington, DC 27
    Prepared statement 29
Lindborg, Hon. Nancy, Assistant Administrator, Bureau of Democracy, Conflict, and Humanitarian Assistance, U.S. Agency for International Development, Washington, DC 12
    Prepared statement 13
Thomas-Greenfield, Hon. Linda, Assistant Secretary of State for African Affairs, U.S. Department of State, Washington, DC 4
    Prepared statement 6

SECURITY AND GOVERNANCE IN SOMALIA: CONSOLIDATING GAINS, CONFRONTING CHALLENGES, AND CHARTING THE PATH FORWARD

TUESDAY, OCTOBER 8, 2013

U.S. SENATE,
SUBCOMMITTEE ON AFRICAN AFFAIRS,
COMMITTEE ON FOREIGN RELATIONS,
Washington, DC.

The subcommittee met, pursuant to notice, at 3 p.m., in room SD–419, Dirksen Senate Office Building, Hon. Christopher A. Coons (chairman of the subcommittee) presiding.

Present: Senators Coons, Flake, and McCain.

OPENING STATEMENT OF HON. CHRISTOPHER A. COONS, U.S. SENATOR FROM DELAWARE

Senator COONS. I am pleased to call to order this hearing of the African Affairs Subcommittee on security and governance issues in Somalia.

Let me at the outset say that in this Government shutdown, I think it remains critical first that we fulfill our constitutional duty in a bipartisan manner to examine ongoing and pressing national security issues. I also think that the shutdown, as we will examine in this hearing, is having a significant and potentially greater impact on our ability to execute effective diplomacy, to provide meaningful development assistance, to analyze intelligence in a timely and thoughtful way in the Horn of Africa and elsewhere. And so I think it is relevant to our current state to have this hearing today, and I am grateful for the cooperation of the full committee chair and ranking and my ranking, Senator Flake, in allowing us to move forward today particularly given the very strong panels of witnesses we have before us.

As we work together to help Somalia chart a course that may lead to a more stable and secure future, I think it is additionally helpful for us to provide a strong example of a functioning democracy that we can be proud of here at home.

I would like to welcome, as I mentioned, Ranking Member Flake and other members of the committee who may join us and our distinguished witnesses on our first panel: Assistant Secretary of State for African Affairs, Linda Thomas-Greenfield; Deputy Assistant Secretary of Defense for Africa, Amanda Dory; and USAID Assistant Administrator for Bureaucracy—excuse me—Democracy——

[Laughter.]

Senator COONS [continuing]. Conflict and Humanitarian Assistance, Nancy Lindborg. Nancy Lindborg is not the Assistant Secretary for Bureaucracy but for Democracy. Forgive me.

On our second panel, we will have Andre Le Sage, senior research fellow for Africa at the National Defense University's Institute for National Strategic Studies; Abdi Aynte, founder and executive director of the Heritage Institute for Policy Studies in Mogadishu. And thank you for the effort involved in your travel here to join us today. And E.J. Hogendoorn, deputy director for Africa at the International Crisis Group.

Thank you to all of our witnesses. I know in several of your cases it was difficult to make preparations, given the shutdown. I am grateful for your cooperation and presence here today.

Today's hearing comes almost exactly two decades after the battle of Mogadishu, in which 18 Americans were killed defending U.S. interests and providing vital humanitarian assistance to Somalia. Following the United States withdrawal that occurred after that and after 20 years of state collapse, lawlessness, and general difficulties in Somalia, recent developments have given us significant reasons to be hopeful. Broad progress in Somalia is due, in no small part, to the security gains made by the African Union mission in Somalia known as AMISOM, consisting of Kenyan, Uganda, Burundian, and other African national troops in coordination with the Ethiopian military. AMISOM has deprived al-Shabaab of territory and revenue creating much-needed space to begin building a functioning state and state structures. This stability has allowed Somalia to form a constituent assembly, an elected new government which was official recognized by the United States last year.

As our witnesses will testify, while much progress has been made, significant challenges still remain. The Somali people are frustrated with the government's failure to provide basic services, education, and health care and others, and the humanitarian situation remains severe. This year, for example, there are more than 2 million Somalis without adequate food access, and recently more than 160 confirmed cases of polio have emerged, just a reminder of the very fragile health and humanitarian situation in Somalia.

Recognizing these matters cannot be fully addressed without a functioning state, the Somali people are impatient with the central government's lack of leadership on forming federal states, as required by the constitution. The government now has 36 months to complete a constitution, conduct a constitutional referendum, and hold national elections. Increased security has provided the foundation for stability and governance, but as the horrific attack in Kenya 2 weeks ago demonstrates, al-Shabaab still is capable of operating both within and beyond Somalia's borders. The unconscionable targeting of innocent civilians by al-Shabaab requires our attention and resources, and as we consider what it means for Somalia, American interests in the region, and our allies in the region, it is worthy of extra attention today. This is why I will soon introduce, along with Senator Flake, a resolution condemning the Westgate attack and reaffirming U.S. support for Kenya and for regional efforts to counter terrorism.

This hearing is an opportunity to consider how U.S. support can help Somalis build on gains in security and governance. Since 2006, our country has provided nearly $700 million of support to AMASOM and the Somali National Army, in addition to the nearly $140 million to support stabilization, democracy, and economic growth in the past 2 years.

Despite these investments, I am concerned our strategy has not fully kept pace with changing realities on the ground, particularly concerns about governance, and I intend to introduce legislation requiring the administration to present its Somalia strategy to Congress with benchmarks for progress and a timeline for implementation, which I hope we can discuss in more detail today.

I am particularly pleased to welcome Assistant Secretary Thomas-Greenfield for her first hearing before our committee before being confirmed to her post and again express gratitude to Mr. Aynte for traveling from Mogadishu to be with us today and to all of our witnesses for the skills, expertise, and background you will bring to this hearing.

With that, I will turn it over to Senator Flake for his opening statement.

Senator.

OPENING STATEMENT OF HON. JEFF FLAKE, U.S. SENATOR FROM ARIZONA

Senator FLAKE. I thank the chairman. I appreciate him holding this hearing and for you making the sacrifice to be here and some challenges with the shutdown and obviously geographical challenges as well. So thank you for being here.

As events of the past weekend indicate, United States interests continue to be threatened in Somalia. Nearly 20 years to the day after the battle of Mogadishu, unfortunately known as ''Blackhawk Down,'' U.S. special forces once again risked their lives in defense of those interests. Yet, 20 years later, it seems that the same problems that plagued Somalia earlier since the collapse of the central government in 1991, and perhaps even before, continue to plague it today.

Today's hearing will provide us with an excellent opportunity to evaluate current United States policy toward the Somali Government, which the U.S. Government recognized for the first time earlier this year. That is significant and we need to make sure that that leads to something positive. It is encouraging that the recognition occurred, but we need to make sure, like I said, that is moving in the right direction.

The security situation and the threat posed by al-Shabaab also need to be assessed, especially in the wake of the Nairobi terror attack in the past couple of weeks.

Lastly, the assistance that the United States provides to Somalia for development and security needs to be examined to ensure the tax dollars spent in Somalia go to support United States objectives there.

This hearing today I feel is important as a first step to help ensuring that in another 20 years we will not be hearing reports of United States special forces risking their lives again in Somalia.

I look forward to hearing from the witnesses today, and again thank you to the chairman for pushing forward on this. I think it is a good show that we are still having hearings and moving forward even with the shutdown. So thank you for being here.

Senator COONS. Thank you, Senator Flake.

And now we will move to our first panel of witnesses. Broadly speaking, we would encourage you to keep opening comments to 5 minutes, but please, we are here to hear from you. So first, if we might, Madam Assistant Secretary.

STATEMENT OF HON. LINDA THOMAS–GREENFIELD, ASSISTANT SECRETARY OF STATE FOR AFRICAN AFFAIRS, U.S. DEPARTMENT OF STATE, WASHINGTON, DC

Ms. THOMAS-GREENFIELD. Good afternoon, Chairman Coons, Ranking Member Flake. It really is my pleasure to appear before you today to talk about Somalia. You reminded me this is my first hearing since taking over my position about 2 months ago, and it really is important for me because, as Assistant Secretary for African Affairs, Somalia will remain a top foreign policy priority for the Department of State as it has for the Obama administration.

This past year marked significant changes in Somalia and in our bilateral relationship with Somalia. The election of President Hassan Sheikh Mohamud was a welcome signal that room for political progress in Somalia was opening. This was made possible in part because of the international community's support for the Djibouti Peace Process and the leadership role of our regional partners, notably the African Union and the Intergovernmental Authority on Development, IGAD. On January 17, we formally recognized the Federal Government of Somalia after two decades of transitional governments. Nonetheless, the U.S. Government also understood very clearly that Somalia would face considerable challenges as it worked to rebuild its statehood.

The successes of the African Union mission in Somalia, AMISOM troop-contributing countries, and strategic partners to combat and eviscerate al-Shabaab are demonstrating the strength of an African-led model. Nonetheless, this Somalia-based al-Qaeda affiliate remains a dangerous presence. The all-too-recent terrorist attack on the Westgate Shopping Mall in Nairobi, for which al-Shabaab has taken credit, is a chilling example of the challenges for Somalia and the region. The attack suggests that violent extremism in the Horn of Africa may be evolving. It also makes clear that al-Shabaab presents a threat to U.S. partner nations in East Africa, to American citizens, and to U.S. interests in that region and elsewhere.

Al-Shabaab must be stopped. The Federal Government of Somalia must increase its capacity to counter al-Shabaab, unify a fractured political system, and provide basic services to the Somali people. For all this, the Government of Somalia needs our support and much more. Our primary interest in Somalia is to help the people of Somalia build a peaceful nation that is stable with a stable government that is able to ensure civil security and services for its citizens.

This leads me to turn to what our policy engagement is in Somalia.

Prior to our recognition of the Federal Government of Somalia, our Somalia policy had three primary elements: provide support for the African Union mission in Somalia, or AMISOM as it is commonly known, and AMISOM's strategic partner Ethiopia, to combat al-Shabaab and provide political space for the government to operate. Second, we wanted to respond to the humanitarian crisis and initiate stabilization where possible. And third, we wanted to promote our dual track policy. This is prior transition.

Post transition, the three elements of our Somali policy have evolved and it is as follows.

First, we continue to support AMISOM as the primary stabilizing force in Somalia, as we expand our assistance to the Somali National Army to build its institutional and operational capacity. From fiscal year 2007 through fiscal year 2013, the United States obligated approximately 512 million U.S. dollars in support of AMISOM, in addition to our assessed contributions for the U.N. logistics support package for AMISOM. During the same period, we obligated more than $170 million to support the Somali National Army to counter al-Shabaab more effectively.

Second, we have shifted focus from humanitarian crisis response, now concentrating on security and stability, laying the foundation for economic recovery through our development-focused programming. In fiscal year 2012 and fiscal year 2013, we provided nearly $140 million in funding to support Somalia's stabilization, democracy, and economic growth activities.

Third, our dual track approach concluded with the successful completion of the Djibouti Peace Process and the recognition of the Federal Government of Somalia. The United States has underscored the importance of outreach and engagement with the regional administrations to form the federal framework. We will continue to fund humanitarian assistance and civil society programs in Somaliland and Puntland with an objective of improving regional collaboration toward federalism.

Our assistance to Somalia includes an emphasis on human rights, on accountability, child soldier prevention, countering human trafficking, and budget transparency and fiscal management.

The tragic and cowardly attack on innocent civilians at Kenya's Westgate Mall has underscored vulnerabilities in the Horn of Africa and demonstrates that al-Shabaab has a capable network in East Africa and it is willing to carry out attacks outside of Somalia. Concerted pressure from AMISOM and the Somali National Army has weakened al-Shabaab's ability to wage conventional military offensives and to hold territory inside Somalia. We attribute this to the success of the African-led model for achieving greater stability in Somalia. However, al-Shabaab is able to conduct destabilizing operations in East Africa.

The Department is working closely with our regional partners on counterterrorism efforts and we are reviewing internally what further resources we can provide to shore up AMISOM and further support their efforts, secure the border of Somalia and its neighbors, and contribute to the international effort to shape the Somali National Army into a cohesive, professional, and effective force.

For the United States to effectively engage on these complex issues, understand local dynamics, build relationships, and manage our expanding programs in Somalia, we eventually need to establish a permanent U.S. diplomatic presence there. Ultimately, it is the security condition in Somalia that will dictate when we can establish a more permanent presence, and we recognize that the time is not right for that at this time. However, we are moving in that direction. Our current posture allows for our Nairobi-based diplomatic team to travel to the Somali capital and other key regions with increased frequency and duration, as security conditions permit.

Building political cooperation among Somali regions and clans in support of the federal framework is essential if democracy, economic growth, and security are truly to take hold in Somalia. This is a message that President Hassan Sheikh emphasized during his Washington meetings with Secretary Kerry, with Secretary Hagel, with National Security Advisor Rice, and with me when I met with him in New York. We see budding signs that Hassan Sheikh is meaningfully engaging regional administrations: the Somalia Federal Government signed the Jubaland Accords on August 22, recognizing that regional entity and mapping a way forward to become a federal state; the federal government introduced a roadmap to the 2016 elections with a focus on political inclusion and security; and Mogadishu and Somaliland came to an agreement on regulating air space, a step toward wider reconciliation.

Ultimately, the development of participatory, accountable, and representative governmental institutions that respond to the needs of the Somali people will secure that country's future. We are committed to working with the government and the people of Somalia to help them realize that vision.

Thank you.

[The prepared statement of Ms. Thomas-Greenfield follows:]

PREPARED STATEMENT OF ASSISTANT SECRETARY LINDA THOMAS-GREENFIELD

INTRODUCTION

Good afternoon, Chairman Coons, Ranking Member Flake, and distinguished members of the mommittee. It is my pleasure to appear before you today to talk about Somalia, which, during my tenure as Assistant Secretary of State for African Affairs, will remain a top foreign policy priority for the Department of State, as it is for the Obama administration. The past year marked significant changes in Somalia and in our bilateral relationship with Somalia. The election of President Hassan Sheikh Mohamud was a welcome signal that room for political progress in Somalia was opening. This was made possible, in part, by the international community's support of the Djibouti Peace Process and the leadership role of our regional partners, notably the African Union and the Intergovernmental Authority on Development (IGAD. On January 17, we formally recognized the Federal Government of Somalia (FGS), after two decades of transitional governments. Nonetheless, the U.S. Government also understood very clearly that Somalia would face considerable challenges as it worked to rebuild its statehood.

The successes of the African Union Mission in Somalia (AMISOM), AMISOM troop-contributing countries, and strategic partners to combat and eviscerate al-Shabaab are demonstrating the strength of an Africa-led model. Nonetheless, this Somalia-based al-Qaeda affiliate remains a dangerous presence. The all-too-recent terrorist attack on the Westgate Shopping Mall in Nairobi, for which al-Shabaab has taken credit, is a chilling example of the challenges for Somalia and the region. This attack suggests that violent extremism in the Horn of Africa may be evolving. It also makes clear that al-Shabaab presents a threat to U.S. partner nations in East Africa, to American citizens, and to U.S. interests. Al-Shabaab must be stopped. The Federal Government of Somalia must increase its capacity to counter al-Shabaab, unify a fractured political system, and provide basic services to the Somali people. For all this, the Government of Somalia needs our support—and much more of it. Our primary interest in Somalia is to help the people of Somalia build a peaceful nation with a stable government, able to ensure civil security and services for its citizens. This in turn will prevent terrorists from using Somali territory as a safe haven.

U.S. POLICY AND ENGAGEMENT IN SOMALIA

Prior to our recognition of the Federal Government of Somalia, our Somalia policy had three primary elements:

> (1) Provide support for the African Union Mission in Somalia, or AMISOM as it is commonly known, and AMISOM's strategic partner Ethiopia, to combat al-Shabaab and provide political space for the government to operate;
> (2) Respond to humanitarian crises and initiate stabilization where possible; and
> (3) Promote our "dual-track" policy.

Post transition, these three elements of our Somali policy have evolved as follows:

- First, we continue to support AMISOM as the primary stabilizing force in Somalia, as we expand our assistance to the Somali National Army to build its institutional and operational capacity. From FY 2007 through FY 2013, the United States obligated approximately $512 million in support of AMISOM, in addition to our assessed contributions for the U.N. logistics support package for AMISOM. During that same period, we obligated more than $170 million to support the Somali National Army to counter al-Shabaab more effectively.
- Second, we have shifted focus from humanitarian crisis response, now concentrating on security and stability, laying the foundation for economic recovery through our development-focused programming. In FY 2012 and FY 2013, we provided nearly $140 million in funding to support Somalia's stabilization, democracy, and economic growth activities.
- Third, our dual-track approach concluded with the successful completion of the Djibouti Peace Process and the recognition of the Federal Government of Somalia. The United States has underscored the importance of outreach and engagement with the regional administrations to form the federal framework. We will continue to fund humanitarian assistance and civil society programs in Somaliland and Puntland, with an objective of improving regional collaboration toward federalism.

Our assistance to Somalia includes an emphasis on human rights and accountability, child soldier prevention, countering human trafficking, and budget transparency and fiscal management.

WESTGATE ATTACK

The tragic and cowardly attack on innocents at Kenya's Westgate Mall has underscored vulnerabilities in the Horn of Africa and demonstrates that al-Shabaab has a capable network in East Africa and is willing to carry out attacks outside Somalia. Concerted pressure from AMISOM and the Somali National Army has weakened al-Shabaab's ability to wage conventional military offensives and to hold territory inside Somalia. We attribute this to the success of the African-led model for achieving greater stability in Somalia. However, al-Shabaab can still conduct destabilizing operations in the East Africa region. The Department is working closely with our regional partners on counterterrorism efforts, and we are reviewing internally what further resources we can shore up to further support AMISOM, secure the borders of Somalia and its neighbors, and contribute to the international effort to shape the Somali National Army into a cohesive, professional, and effective force.

U.S. PRESENCE

For the United States to effectively engage on these complex issues, understand local dynamics, build relationships, and manage our expanding programs in Somalia, we eventually need to establish a permanent U.S. diplomatic presence in Somalia. Ultimately, it is the security conditions in Somalia that will dictate when we can establish a more permanent presence and we recognize that the time is not right to do this. However, we are moving in that direction. Our current posture allows for our Nairobi-based diplomatic team to travel into the Somali capital and other key regions with increased frequency and duration, as security conditions permit.

FEDERALISM/POLITICAL COOPERATION

Building political cooperation among Somali regions and clans in support of the federal framework is essential, if democracy, economic growth, and security are truly to take hold in Somalia. This is a message that President Hassan Sheikh emphasized during his Washington meetings with Secretary Kerry, Secretary Hagel, and National Security Advisor Rice. We see budding signs that Hassan Sheikh is meaningfully engaging regional administrations: The Somali Federal Government signed the Jubbaland Accords on August 22, recognizing the regional entity and mapping a way forward to become a federal state; the Federal Government introduced a roadmap to the 2016 elections with a focus on political inclusion and security; and Mogadishu and Somaliland came to an agreement on regulating air-space, a step towards wider reconciliation.

CONCLUSION

Ultimately, the development of participatory, accountable, and representative governmental institutions that respond to the needs of the Somali people will secure the country's future. We are committed to work with the Government and people of Somalia to help them realize this vision.

Senator COONS. Thank you very much, Madam Assistant Secretary, and I look forward to a round of questions on the topic.

If I might, next Deputy Assistant Secretary Dory. We look forward to your testimony.

STATEMENT OF AMANDA DORY, DEPUTY ASSISTANT SECRETARY FOR AFRICAN AFFAIRS, U.S. DEPARTMENT OF DEFENSE, WASHINGTON, DC

Ms. DORY. Chairman Coons, Ranking Member Flake, distinguished members of the subcommittee, and staff, thank you for the opportunity to appear today to update you on the Department of Defense's role vis-a-vis Somalia and the way ahead there.

The United States, as you know, has not maintained an official military relationship with Somalia since the early 1990s, in large part because there was not a United States-recognized Government of Somalia until 2013.

In light of the recognition in January 2013, the Department of Defense, in close cooperation and coordination with the State Department, seeks to develop a normalized military-to-military relationship with the Somali National Security Forces, SNSF.

Somalia is emerging from 20 years of civil war, as all have acknowledged. Since 2006, al-Shabaab has led a violent insurgency in southern and central Somalia, first against the former transitional federal government and now against the Federal Government of Somalia and African Union Mission in Somalia—AMISOM—forces. Once controlling most major Somali cities, al-Shabaab operated with impunity.

Today, Somali, AMISOM, and Ethiopian forces have weakened al-Shabaab as a conventional fighting force in Somalia. However, al-Shabaab is still dangerous and capable of conducting sophisticated, unconventional attacks to disrupt AMISOM operations and the Somali Government. Recent events in Mogadishu and Nairobi are sobering reminders. Thus, for the foreseeable future, we must maintain focus on Somalia to sustain security progress made to date, as al-Shabaab is likely to remain the primary threat to Somalia and East African stability for some time to come.

The significant gains achieved by Somali and AMISOM forces over the past few years have been critical in providing space for the political process that resulted in Somalia's transition to government now officially recognized. Somalia faces many challenges ahead, but it is moving forward on a positive path that was hard to imagine 5 years ago. As military-to-military relations mature and are normalized with Somalia, DOD, through U.S. Africa Command, will work with the State Department to design security cooperation activities to assist with the development of a unified Somali security force.

There have also been tremendous gains at sea. In and around the Horn of Africa, piracy has virtually been eliminated. As a maritime nation, the United States relies on the unhindered use and access of the seas to ensure our economic well-being. As recently as 2011, Somali pirates held nearly 600 mariner hostages aboard 28 captured ships and roamed an area the size of the United States. Today, thanks to changes in business practices by the commercial maritime industry and the presence of international naval forces, piracy is almost nonexistent off the coast of Somalia.

DOD's approach to the region and to Somalia reflects the U.S. national security strategy, the strategy vis-a-vis sub-Saharan Africa, and the Defense Strategic Guidance. DOD focuses in particular on advancing peace and security by working with partners to address security threats of shared concern and to create an environment that enables improved governance and sustainable broad-based development.

Looking forward, DOD will work, in conjunction with the State Department and other U.S. Government agencies, to provide security assistance to build the capacity of Somalia's security institutions, including their ability to counter terrorism, secure borders and coastline, and reinforcing democratic values and the rule of law. Additionally, we will continue to work with the State Department to support AMISOM and its troop-contributing countries in their efforts to counter and defeat al-Shabaab.

AMISOM represents an important success story in which African forces from Uganda, Burundi, Kenya, Djibouti, and Sierra Leone have collaborated to progressively regain territory from al-Shabaab, working in collaboration with the Somali National Army, as well as Ethiopian forces. The United States and other international partners have provided critical training and equipment assistance to facilitate these efforts.

Once appropriations are approved for the Department of Defense, fiscal year 2014 would be the first in 20 years in which DOD is able to support Somali National Security Forces directly with title 10 activities.

DOD has put in place a senior military representative at the Somali Affairs Unit in Nairobi, who performs a role similar to that of a defense attaché, and we will increase our presence in Mogadishu in tandem with the State Department.

DOD personnel are now participating in both the Joint Security Committee led by the Somali Government and the Somalia Defense Working Group led by the United Nations on a regular basis. Moreover, we have made a concerted effort to increase our key leader engagements with senior Somali officials. This summer, the commander of USAFRICOM, General Rodriguez, made his initial visit to Mogadishu. Additionally, Secretary Hagel hosted the President of Somalia and his Chief of Defense at the Pentagon at the end of September. These face-to-face engagements have been critical in identifying and better understanding Somalia's security needs and concerns.

In conclusion, Somalia will continue to present a complex and fluid set of challenges and opportunities. However, with sustained assistance from the United States and other international partners, Somalia's national security apparatus will be better positioned to fend off the al-Shabaab insurgency and gradually transform the fragile state into a success story.

Thank you for your enduring support to our men and women in uniform and our dedicated team of civilian professionals. We look forward to working with you on Somalia and the other elements of our Africa policy.

Thank you.

[The prepared statement of Ms. Dory follows:]

PREPARED STATEMENT OF DEPUTY ASSISTANT SECRETARY AMANDA J. DORY,

Mr. Chairman, Ranking Member, and distinguished members of the Senate Foreign Relations Committee, thank you for this opportunity to update the subcommittee on the Department of Defense's (DOD) vision and role in Somalia.

INTRODUCTION

The United States has not held an official military relationship with Somalia since the early 1990s, in large part because there was not a U.S.-recognized Government of Somalia until 2013.

In light of the January 2013 recognition of the Federal Government of Somalia, the Department of Defense, in cooperation and close coordination with the Department of State (DOS), seeks to develop a normalized military-to-military relationship with the Somali National Security Forces (SNSF). Both agencies intend to work together in assisting Somalia to build the operational capacity of the SNSF and support the development of Somali security institutions.

SECURITY ENVIRONMENT

Somalia is emerging from 20 years of civil war and the oppressive control of al-Shabaab. Since 2006, al-Shabaab has led a violent insurgency in southern and central Somalia, first against the former Somali Transitional Federal Government, and now against the Federal Government of Somalia and African Union Mission in Somalia (AMISOM) forces. Once controlling most major Somali cities, al-Shabaab operated with impunity.

Today, Somali, AMISOM, and Ethiopian forces have weakened al-Shabaab as a conventional fighting force in Somalia. However, al-Shabaab is still dangerous and capable of conducting sophisticated unconventional attacks to disrupt AMISOM operations and the Somali Government. Recent events in Mogadishu and Nairobi are sobering reminders. Thus, for the foreseeable future, we must maintain focus on Somalia to sustain security progress made to date, as al-Shabaab is likely to remain the primary threat to Somalia and East Africa stability for some time to come.

The significant gains achieved by Somali and AMISOM forces over the past few years have been critical in providing space for the political process that resulted in Somalia's transition to a government now officially recognized by the United States. Somalia faces many challenges ahead, but it is moving forward on a positive path that was hard to imagine 5 years ago. As military-to-military relations mature and are normalized with Somalia, DOD through U.S. Africa Command (USAFRICOM) will work with the DOS to design security cooperation activities to assist with the development of a unified Somali security force.

There have also been tremendous gains at sea. In and around the Horn of Africa, piracy has virtually been eliminated. As a maritime nation, the United States relies on the unhindered use of the seas to ensure our economic well-being, and we seek to ensure the same freedoms for other nations. As recently as 2011, Somali pirates held nearly 600 mariners hostages aboard 28 captured ships, and roamed an area the size of the United States looking for their next opportunity. Today, thanks to changes in business practices by the commercial maritime industry, and the presence of international naval forces, piracy is almost nonexistent off the coast of Somalia. The last successful hijacking of a major commercial ship was in May 2012.

DOD SECURITY ASSISTANCE /COOPERATION

DOD's approach to the region and to Somalia reflects the U.S. National Security Strategy, the U.S. Strategy toward sub-Saharan Africa, Presidential Policy Directive 23 on Security Sector Assistance (SSA), and the Defense Strategic Guidance. DOD focuses in particular on advancing peace and security by working with partners to address security threats of shared concern and to create an environment that enables improved governance and sustainable broad-based development.

Looking forward, DOD will work, in conjunction with the DOS and other U.S. agencies providing security sector assistance to build the capacity of Somali security institutions in pursuit of the following objectives: (1) improve Somalia's ability to counter terrorism and secure its borders and coastline, and (2) reinforce democratic values and respect for rule of law. Additionally, we will continue to work with the State Department to support AMISOM and its troop-contributing countries in their efforts to counter and defeat al-Shabaab, creating space for the extension of governance throughout Somalia's territory. AMISOM represents an important success story in which African forces—from Uganda, Burundi, Kenya, Djibouti, and Sierra Leone—have collaborated to progressively regain territory from al-Shabaab, working in collaboration with the Somali National Army as well as Ethiopian forces. The United States and other international partners have provided critical training and equipment assistance to facilitate the efforts of these forces.

Once appropriations are approved for the Department, fiscal year 2014 (FY 2014) would be the first in 20 years in which DOD is able to support the SNSF directly with title 10 funding. Accordingly, USAFRICOM is working closely with Combined Joint Task Force-Horn of Africa (CJTF–HOA) and DOS to ensure all proposed security cooperation programs are complementary to other ongoing U.S. Government and international efforts and are consistent with all laws affecting U.S. assistance, including the Child Soldiers Prevention Act. Initial training proposals for FY 2014 will likely focus on logistics, personnel management, finance and budgeting, and maintenance, all of which were requested by the Somali leadership.

DOD has put in place a Senior Military Representative at the Somali Affairs Unit in Nairobi, who performs a role similar to a Defense Attaché, and we will increase our presence in Mogadishu in tandem with the State Department. CJTF–HOA personnel are now participating in both the Joint Security Committee led by the Somali Government and the Somalia Defense Working Group led by the United Nations on a regular basis. Moreover, we have made a concerted effort to increase our key leader engagements with senior Somali officials. This summer, the Commander of USAFRICOM made an initial visit to Mogadishu. Additionally, Secretary Hagel recently hosted the President of Somalia, Hassan Sheikh Mohamud and his Chief of Defense, General Elmi, at the Pentagon. These face-to-face engagements have been critical in identifying and better understanding Somali security needs and concerns.

With regard to maritime security, DOD has played and is playing a significant role in countering piracy and maritime crime. In 2009, we established Combined Task Force 151 (CTF–151) in a dedicated effort to prevent further attacks in the Gulf of Aden and off the eastern coast of Somalia. The United States has both commanded this Task Force and provided naval forces to it. In addition to CTF–151, the U.S. Navy also participates in NATO's counterpiracy efforts in the Horn of Africa, as part of Operation Ocean Shield. Today, pirates no longer roam freely. However, notwithstanding the positive trends of the past 2 years, the decline in piracy is perishable if these measures are not maintained.

Finally, DOD and DOS will explore opportunities to increase the SNSF border security capabilities; assist Somalia's maritime security capacity; build a Somali counterterrorism capability to deal with terrorists threats; and assisting in justice sector reforms.

CONCLUSION

Somalia will continue to present a complex and fluid set of challenges and opportunities. However, with sustained assistance from the United States and other international partners, Somalia's national security apparatus will be better positioned to fend off the al-Shabaab insurgency and gradually transform the fragile state into a success story.

Thank you for your enduring support to our men and women in uniform, and our dedicated team of civilian professionals. We look forward to working with you in the months ahead.

Senator COONS. Thank you very much.

Last on our first panel, Assistant Administrator Lindborg, please.

STATEMENT OF HON. NANCY LINDBORG, ASSISTANT ADMINIS-TRATOR, BUREAU OF DEMOCRACY, CONFLICT, AND HUMAN-ITARIAN ASSISTANCE, U.S. AGENCY FOR INTERNATIONAL DEVELOPMENT, WASHINGTON, DC

Ms. LINDBORG. Good afternoon. Thank you, Chairman Coons and Ranking Member Flake. I really appreciate the opportunity to speak with you today and most importantly appreciate your ongoing support for our assistance programs that make a difference in the lives of millions around the world.

I last testified in front of this committee about Somalia in August 2011, and that was as the worst drought in East Africa in 60 years had plunged more than 13 million people in the region into crisis and just after the July 20th U.N. declaration of famine in Somalia. At the height of that crisis, 4 million Somalis' survival depended on receiving emergency assistance, and although the entire region suffered, only in Somalia did the drought result in famine. As noted, it was the deadly combination of drought, 20 years of conflict, a failed state, and the presence of armed terrorists that led to the death of hundreds of thousands of Somalis. And as Amartya Sen has famously said, famines do not happen in democracies.

So 2 years later, it is a remarkable story that we are telling right now, that Somalia has its first legitimate central government since 1991. It has a democratically elected President and Parliament. And I am very pleased to report that just recently I was in Brussels where 58 countries gathered in support of a compact for Somalia that focuses not on famine, but on peace and prosperity. The recent, very tragic al-Shabaab attack in Nairobi underscores the need to reaffirm our commitment to helping Somalia on its pathway to peace and prosperity and economic growth and providing alternatives to violent extremism.

Since 1991, USAID's work in Somalia has been defined by a prolonged, complex humanitarian emergency. However, over the past 5 years with increasing security gains, USAID has been able to increase our support in five key areas for transition, and most importantly in 2012, USAID's democracy and governance efforts supported the formation of Somalia's first national government in 22 years. With other donors, we provided logistics support, constitutional experts to help convene traditional elders and representatives from a cross section of Somali society into a constituent assembly. USAID partners mounted a massive civic education campaign to mobilize support for the constitution drafting process and its eventual adoption by the constituent assembly. This assembly elected new members of Parliament who then selected the new President, Hassan Sheikh Mohamud, through a democratic process.

Globally we see that the greatest poverty and insecurity persists in weak and fragile states that are plagued by stubborn conflict. In 2011, a group of 19 self-identified conflict-affected and fragile states established a new framework for helping countries climb out of protracted conflict called the ''New Deal for Engagement in Fragile States.'' This new deal calls for a clear focus on five key peace-building and state-building goals, including legitimate politics, security, justice, economic foundations, and revenues and services. The compact that we all just endorsed in Brussels with the Government of Somalia sets us on a roadmap to achieve those goals with very clear benchmarks: a federal constitution by 2015; credible elections by 2016; 30 percent quota for women's participation; state security institutions; and so forth. The new deal hinges firmly on mutual accountability and a state-society relationship that is based on inclusion and on dialogue. This very specifically means involving previously marginalized populations, broad civil society consultations, and vital dialogue with regional entities like Somaliland and Puntland. This approach recognizes that security, development, and governance are deeply intertwined and must be pursued together.

Today food insecurity levels in Somalia are at the lowest point since before the 2011 drought. Yet, three key challenges remain. These food security gains are very fragile. We have ongoing humanitarian needs with 870,000 people still in crisis; insecurity, as al-Shabaab and other armed groups continue to limit access; and thirdly, access, which is vital to carrying out both continuing humanitarian efforts and expanding our development actions.

Finally, Somalia is challenged not only by conflict and weak governance but also with the severe weather shocks that are coming in ever-faster cycles. So it is impossible for communities to escape these cycles of crisis. As we have done in other parts of the Horn and in the Sahel, USAID is focused not just on saving lives but building resilience so communities are better prepared for, and able to recover from, the next shock like the drought of 2011.

Ultimately, the Somali people must be the primary architects of peace, democracy, and development in their country, and Somalia would not have the opportunity that it has today were it not for the many members of the Somali community in and outside of the country who are making a daily decision to focus on a future built on hope and peace rather than on conflict and despair. We know the road is long. The challenges are steep this will not be fast nor will it be easy, but with the specific commitments of the new deal, that roadmap, with the specific commitments and continued focus by the people and the Government of Somalia, we believe that right now represents the best chance for peace in two decades and the United States will remain a committed partner.

Thank you again and I look forward to questions.

[The prepared statement of Ms. Lindborg follows:]

PREPARED STATEMENT OF ASSISTANT ADMINISTRATOR NANCY LINDBORG

Good afternoon and thank you, Chairman Coons, Ranking Member Flake, and members of the Senate Foreign Relations Committee's Subcommittee on African Affairs for the opportunity to speak with you today about the complex state of governance, development, and security in Somalia. Thank you also for your continued support for our assistance programs that make a difference in the lives of millions every day.

14

INTRODUCTION

In 2011, the worst drought in East Africa in 60 years plunged more than 13.3 million people into crisis. USAID and the international community's response to the devastating Horn of Africa crisis helped meet the needs of 4.6 million people across the region. Despite these efforts, in July 2011, the United Nations declared famine in two areas of southern Somalia. Additional areas slipped into famine in the weeks to follow and at the height of the crisis, 4 million Somali lives depended on receiving emergency assistance.

While the drought affected millions across the region, only in Somalia did drought result in famine. This is not a designation we use lightly, as it means that at least 20 percent of households face an extreme lack of food with evidence of starvation, death, and destitution; more than 30 percent are acutely malnourished; and the mortality rate exceeds two deaths per 10,000 people a day. In Somalia, it was the deadly combination of drought, 20 years of conflict, a failed state, and the presence of armed terrorists that led to the deaths of hundreds of thousands Somalis. As Amartya Sen famously said, famines don't happen in democracies.

Now, 2 years later, Somalia has its first effective central government since 1991, with democratically elected President Hassan Sheikh Mohamud and a new Somali Federal Parliament. Somalis have worked hard to establish the foundation of their state based on significant efforts to forge a national consensus. And I am very pleased to report that I recently returned from an international meeting on Somalia focused on peace and prosperity, not famine. In Brussels on September 16, 58 countries and 11 international organizations gathered in support of a compact that outlines a roadmap forward. Emerging from 20 years of conflict will be a long and bumpy road, but Somalia is now heading in the right direction, with the best chance in 20 years to move toward a better future.

Today I am pleased to talk to you about this opportunity, the new frameworks and international partnerships in support of Somalia, and what USAID is doing to help Somalia transition out of conflict, fragility, and chronic poverty.

The recent, tragic al-Shabaab attack in Nairobi only underscores the need for the international community to reaffirm our commitment to assist the development of a more legitimate, inclusive democracy in Somalia. This will be central to peace, prosperity, economic growth, and to providing positive alternatives to violent extremism in those communities most at risk of recruitment and radicalization to violence.

EMERGING FROM TWO DECADES OF CONFLICT

USAID's work in Somalia for the last two decades has been defined by a prolonged complex humanitarian emergency and significant security constraints. Since 1991, widespread and persistent food insecurity, civil strife, interclan conflict, political instability, endemic poverty, and recurrent cycles of flooding and drought have resulted in severe humanitarian needs. For decades weak governance and insecurity have inhibited meaningful solutions and prevented humanitarian aid from reaching many who need it most.

However, over the last 5 years, enabled by security advancements made by the U.N. Security Council authorized African Union Mission in Somalia (AMISOM), USAID has increased support focused on three areas critical for transition: stronger ties between government and community; economic opportunity through improved government-private sector relations; and improved government ability to provide basic services.

Most importantly, in 2012, USAID's democracy and governance efforts supported the formation of Somalia's first national government in 22 years. USAID and other international development partners provided logistics support and constitutional experts to help convene traditional elders and representatives from a cross-section of Somali society in a Constituent Assembly. This Assembly elected new Members of Parliament, who then selected President Hassan Sheikh Mohamud through a democratic process. USAID partners mounted a massive civic education campaign to mobilize support for the constitution-drafting process and its eventual adoption by the Constituent Assembly.

THE NEW DEAL FOR ENGAGEMENT IN FRAGILE STATES: A WAY FORWARD FOR SOMALIA

Globally, we are seeing that the greatest poverty and insecurity persists in those states plagued by weak and fragile governments and stubborn conflict. These environments require a distinct approach. In 2011, a group of 19 self-identified "conflict affected and fragile states," working with development partners and international organizations, identified a new framework for helping countries climb out of protracted conflict called the New Deal for Engagement in Fragile States. The New Deal calls for a clear focus on five key peace-building and state-building goals: legitimate politics, security, justice, economic foundations, and revenues and services. Based on research by the World Bank, this approach recognizes that security, development, and governance are deeply intertwined.

The New Deal calls on Somali Government officials, international donors, and civil society to work together to create a common plan. It hinges firmly on the notion of mutual accountability and a commitment by both fragile states and their international partners to build mutual trust by providing aid and managing resources more effectively and aligning these resources for results.

Since 2013, with the consolidation of the Somali Central Government and a new committed government partner, USAID has been working closely with international development partners to apply the New Deal in Somalia. Just last month in Brussels, together with our colleagues at the State Department, international development partners, and Somali President Hassan Sheikh Mohamud, we endorsed the terms of a compact focused on moving all stakeholders toward shared state-building and peace-building goals. This plan includes benchmarks for success and roles and responsibilities with clear leadership by the Government of Somalia.

Fostering a strong state-society relationship, inclusion, and dialogue are all key elements of this effort; in Somalia this means involving previously marginalized populations and vital dialogue between the Government in Mogadishu and regional entities like Somaliland and Puntland. Planning endeavors must be given the necessary time, enabling outreach to regional stakeholders and civil society. This is key to participatory democracy. We understand that such consultations are time-sensitive, but it will be time well-spent. By their nature, consultations often generate a wide range of opinions regarding the best way forward, which helps leaders chart effective solutions with buy-in from the people.

The Compact sets forth the intent of the Government of Somalia and the international community to work together to achieve vital priorities including: finalizing and adopting a federal constitution by December 2015, holding credible elections by 2016, fulfilling a 30-percent quota for women's participation in representative bodies, strengthening the capacity of state security institutions to provide basic safety and security, and implementing a national program for the treatment and handling of disengaged combatants. Importantly, it commits donor participants to provide aid in a conflict-sensitive manner, which is crucial given Somalia's complex conflict history and dynamics.

USAID's ongoing democracy and governance work is already helping to make progress toward these goals by supporting Parliament's capacity-building and engagement with civil society as well as the use of financial software systems to improve revenue collection and promote accountability.

The last 20 years in Somalia have demonstrated just how fragile the state-building process can be. In Somalia, we all know that the road is long and challenges remain steep, but with its specific commitments, and committed partners, we believe the New Deal represents the best chance for peace and development in two decades.

CONTINUING CHALLENGES

Today, food insecurity levels in Somalia are at the lowest point since before the 2010–11 drought. However, insecurity, lack of access, and ongoing humanitarian needs remain key challenges. These recent food security gains are very fragile with 870,000 people still in crisis and another 2.3 million people on the brink of falling back into crisis. Malnutrition levels remain elevated, with roughly 206,000 children under the age of 5 acutely malnourished; more than 1.1 million people are internally displaced, primarily in southern and central Somalia, in addition to the 1 million Somali refugees in the region.

Recent violence—including intercommunal violence in Kismayo town, surrounding areas of Lower Juba Region, and in and around Mogadishu—underscore the ongoing insecurity challenges throughout the country.

Moreover, without consistent government control over rural areas, armed groups will likely continue to limit access for humanitarian and development workers. Al-Shabaab and other violent extremist groups continue to interfere with relief operations in rural areas across southern Somalia, including in Middle Juba Region and parts of Bakool, Bay, and Gedo regions. The withdrawal of the Ethiopian National Defense Force from Bay Region's capital city of Baidoa may further restrict humanitarian access and result in additional population displacement. Similarly, increasing security efforts by the Kenya Defense Forces may have access implications in

Kismayo and reignite tensions in the community. Access will be vital to carrying out both continuing humanitarian efforts and expanding development activities.

BUILDING RESILIENCE

With climate change, we know severe weather shocks are coming even faster, making it even more impossible for the poorest communities to escape a vicious cycle of crisis. We are bringing our development and humanitarian teams together for joint analysis and planning toward the shared goal of strengthening resilience to make communities, institutions, and society as a whole better prepared for and able to recover from shocks such as the drought and famine of 2011 and 2012.

For example, humanitarian activities supporting pastoralist livelihoods are linking up with long-term economic growth efforts focused on animal health and livestock production. USAID's Resilience Agenda—an effort to do business differently and more closely coordinate with international partners to help vulnerable communities escape cycles of crisis—and the New Deal framework share the goals of improving livelihoods, generating employment, fostering inclusive growth and conflict management. Importantly, good governance is at the center of both comprehensive approaches.

CONCLUSION

For Somalia to break free of recurrent violence, stabilization activities must be supported by political actors, civil society members, and a Somali population committed to a comprehensive peace-building process that ensures widespread participation but also emphasizes reconciliation over narrow interests. Ultimately, the primary architects of what peace, democracy, and development efforts look like must be the Somali people. Somalia would not have the kind of opportunity it has today were it not for the many members of the Somali community who make a daily decision to focus on a future built on hope and peace rather than on conflict and despair. And the United States remains a committed partner.

Senator COONS. Thank you very much.

I think we will do 7-minute rounds, if we might.

Thank you very much to all the members of the first panel for your testimony and frankly for starting by focusing on the enormous progress that has been made in the last 2 years since you first testified, Assistant Administrator Lindborg, a reminder that there has been real progress in dealing with the famine and the humanitarian crisis, in dealing with piracy which has been dramatically curtailed, and in making steady progress toward a legitimate state recognized by the United States and laying the platform for progress toward a federal-state structure and toward moving forward with dealing with some of the unresolved constitutional issues. Significant progress.

I would like to ask first of all three of you, if I might, what impact is the current federal government shutdown having on your ability, your departments' abilities or stations' abilities to review and approve programs, to carry out and deliver needed development, diplomacy, intelligence, or other defense-related services, and were this shutdown to continue for another few weeks, would those impacts strengthen or become more pronounced in any way? Please, if you might.

Ms. THOMAS-GREENFIELD. If I may start. Thank you very much for that question. And I think I can say and I am sure my colleagues will agree that the shutdown has had an enormous impact on our ability to coordinate foreign policy within the interagency framework as some of our colleagues within the interagency are on furlough and they are not available for us to coordinate with or speak with. And it is really important, if we are to have an interagency process, that everyone is at the table.

We are also not in a position to travel. In the case of travel to Somalia, that is a two-sided problem because of security now—our people are not traveling, but had there not been a security issue, they still could not travel because we have a travel moratorium.

And then, thirdly, our Ambassadors are not able to host events that build on the critical relationships that we need to develop to do our jobs.

I think an important part is we are not able to monitor our assistance. Senator Flake mentioned the large amount of taxpayer dollars that are supporting Somalia. We feel responsible for those taxpayer dollars, and in order to ensure that those dollars are going to where they need to go, we need to be able to get out in the field and monitor, and the shutdown will certainly impact that as well.

Senator COONS. Ms. Dory.

Ms. DORY. Similarly to the areas laid out by my colleague, I would just add from DOD's perspective, civilian employees in particular for the first week of the shutdown were affected and that significantly diminished our ability to operate across the Department in all key areas, whether it was acquisition, personnel readiness and training, policy development, et cetera, et cetera.

There are also kind of unexpected ways where the shutdown impacts, for example, the inability to make cash expenditures. That could be fine as far as if you are thinking about cash expenditures to entertain a visiting delegation, for example, that perhaps that could be set to the side temporarily. But when it comes to aircraft who are paying fees of various kinds, whether it is refueling in overseas locations and you are unable to expend cash, that is just a very small example of the limitation imposed by the shutdown.

And then perhaps most fundamentally is just the absence of understanding for fiscal year 2014 what our planning levels are to work with and that impedes on the longer term business in the Somalia context, for example, what title 10 DOD resources and title 22 State Department resources will be available to be brought to bear, whether it is vis-a-vis Somalia or any of the other countries in the region.

Senator COONS. Ms. Lindborg.

Ms. LINDBORG. I would just add to that. We are in a really critical time as we move toward these important milestones that will be critical for seizing this moment for helping Somalia move forward. This is an effort that the United States is doing in close partnership with the international community. There are a number of important meetings that we are constrained in being able to participate in right now. At a moment where we want to be at the table to talk about the importance of accountable transparent governance and of a functioning government, we are not able to be there in addition to the constraints to our travel and our ability to work with the interagency because of furloughs.

Senator COONS. Several of you mentioned that this particular structure, AMISOM, is in some ways a model of African-led regional security being successful. I would be interested in each of your respective spheres sort of how you see that model playing out going forward. What are the lessons learned, strengths, weaknesses? I have represented in a number of settings that this is something we really ought to be looking to more broadly where we have a number of different nations coming together operationally driving al-Shabaab out of significant swaths of the country, stabilizing the security of the country, making possible development, improved security, improved statecraft. Overall, frankly, it has gotten very little attention in the domestic U.S. press, but compared to what was the condition in Somalia a year or 2 ago, this has been a truly outstanding success of a model that is AU-chaired and African-led. So I would be interested, if you might, Madam Secretary, what you see as the lessons learned, the strengths and weaknesses, and what we should be expecting going forward for the AMISOM mission. And then each of you in turn.

Ms. THOMAS-GREENFIELD. Thank you very much for that question.

And I do think the AMISOM model is a model that can be used. Some of the lessons, as I look back on this in my limited time in this office, but with much experience on the continent, is, I think, we have to do a better job of ensuring that we provide the support that AMISOM needs to do its job. While at the UNGA in New York, I met with the Foreign Minister of Uganda, and he said we have the people to put on the ground, but we still need the support to move those people around. We need the enablers. And because of our budget cycles and how we budget, we are not always able to provide them with that support as early as they need that support. We also want to be able to continue to support them, and each year, because of our funding cycles, sometimes there is a delay in when we can get our support out to them.

You talk about how we might use this model. A similar model was used in Mali where I was a few weeks ago for the inauguration of the new President of Mali. In less than 18 months, we were able to bring that country back into a democratic country moving forward because of an African-led process supported by us.

Thank you.

Senator COONS. And what sort of lessons might we learn about the stabilization and the transfer of security function from 11 to the Somali National Forces, Assistant Secretary Dory?

Ms. DORY. I think as we look at the success of AMISOM—and there are many successes associated with it—one of the challenges is just the pulling together all of the external supporters with all of the different coalition of the willing that the troop contributing countries who step up and answer the call and just managing across that complexity is one of the biggest challenges and can make things slower and less efficient than otherwise would be the case.

I do think you are seeing replication of the model in other locations because it is successful, whether it is countering the Lord's Resistance Army that we have talked about in other contexts where you have the United States and other enabling regional partners taking the lead to pursue the Lord's Resistance Army, a similar model in the Mali context where you had regional forces first in the African-led International Support Mission to Mali —AFISMA—configuration and now as a U.N. mission, that are being supported by external parties as well. So I think the replication is an indicator of the success.

Our part is really bringing the targeted training capacity and bringing in enablers, as Assistant Secretary Thomas-Greenfield referred to. Sometimes that can be quite challenging, especially in the area of logistics, which is the true shortfall when you look across the many different missions on the African Continent, both the logistics capabilities of African partners themselves and then the tools with which we are able to support them.

Thank you.

Senator COONS. Building on airlift capacity is, I think, a long-term goal we all share.

And if I might, just in conclusion, Assistant Administrator Lindborg, how do you see AMISOM's success in terms of stabilization and security contributing to the development picture you mentioned in your testimony, that they are inextricably intertwined?

Ms. LINDBORG. Absolutely. Somalia is a perfect example of how one needs security for development but also how development leads to greater security. And so as we continue to push our development programs into south-central Somalia, the opportunity is to help citizens gain greater confidence in both local and central governing structures and to receive the services that are absolutely essential for their well-being and for their support for the way forward. This is supported by greater security. So it is a hand-in-hand proposition that going forward will be important that we are able to realize the gains from both security and development working together for peace and prosperity.

Senator COONS. Thank you.

Senator Flake.

Senator FLAKE. Thank you. Thank you all.

Continuing on AMISOM, I was just looking at a map provided by the Atlantic Council in terms of the area of the country controlled by government forces and whatever, and it is pretty small. Ms. Dory, can you explain how far out of Mogadishu does the government's writ actually go? I mean, how much are we actually controlling outside through AMISOM or the security forces there?

Ms. DORY. Right. So what AMISOM has succeeded in doing essentially is taking away the revenue generation prospects for al-Shabaab that were related to the port operations in both Mogadishu and Kismayo. So in focusing first on those population centers and liberating them from al-Shabaab, that was a critical step taken in terms of weakening their sustainment capabilities. As you have seen on the map, the forces have since pushed out of both of those population centers farther into the countryside, but there are swaths of Somali territory that are not under effective control of the central government at this point. And there are corridors in between, some of the major centers that are maintained and patrolled by AMISOM. But it is quite clear that there remains additional territory that is available to al-Shabaab as a sanctuary, and that is really the work ahead both with AMISOM and with the Somali National Army to continue to pressure al-Shabaab so that they continue to fracture and continually are displaced from the locations that they are currently occupying such as Barawe which we saw over the weekend is a current node for al-Shabaab.

Senator FLAKE. Is AMISOM engaged in counterinsurgency activities at all, or is that just the security forces?

Ms. DORY. AMISOM is pursuing al-Shabaab directly alongside the Somali National Security Services. So they are enabling one another. At various times, one takes the lead or the other takes the lead. But in the vast majority of operations, they are operating together.

Senator FLAKE. And in 2010, the AU wanted to change the role of AMISOM from peacekeeping to peace enforcement, and that was objected to by the United Nations. Is that a distinction without a difference, or does that matter?

Ms. DORY. I think that refers to the rules of engagement that they are operating under, and AMISOM at this point is operating with robust rules of engagement where they are not a defensive force, they are an offensive force. They are making peace.

Senator FLAKE. Now, is the transition happening quickly enough in terms of turning over the security functions to the country's security forces?

Ms. DORY. In my view, the transition is happening as quickly as it can, which by definition is slowly because the ability of the Somali National Army to actually take over is quite constrained at this point. The Somali National Army is about 17,000 strong at this point based on the count from their chief of defense, General Elmi, but of that force, many are militia forces or other individuals who are under the banner of the Somali National Army, some of whom have been trained. Many have not. They have been trained by a variety of external sources. So there are some major capability gaps as far as the Somali National Army's ability to step in for AMISOM. And I think we would forecast that it will be a period of time before the SNA is ready to step up and take over the mission currently performed by AMISOM.

Senator FLAKE. Ms. Lindborg, you were talking about the government there. You mentioned that the Parliament is democratically elected, as well as the President or you referenced them as democratically elected. Is it not more of an appointment there by tribal elders? And then the President is then elected by the MPs. But how much of an election is it for the Parliament, and how much legitimacy do they have going forward?

To preface that, there was some criticism. I think the Economist wrote a year ago or so that some of the MP slots were going for about $25,000, and there was some corruption alleged. Can you talk about that and how we are moving away from that or what legitimacy the government has going forward?

Ms. LINDBORG. Yes. There have definitely been challenges of corruption in Somalia through the years. The importance is the commitment of the current government to move beyond that as they look at that list of benchmarks with the elections and the new constitution over the next several years. It is a 36-month timetable.

There is historically a great deal of factionalism within Somalia that will be important to have the kind of inclusive dialogue over the next 36 months to find a way forward that enables that kind of participation in the solution. This is one of the best opportunities that Somalia has had in two decades with an inclusive process, and that kind of planning will have to continue where you bring in regional entities and you bring in a lot of the local governments that have been critical for holding communities together over the last several decades but now need to come together under an umbrella of the central government or a federated government.

Senator FLAKE. The President was elected by the Parliament. The Parliament was elected or appointed? The current Parliament.

Ms. LINDBORG. It was selected by this assembly process, and then, yes, they selected the President. And as we gear toward the 2016 Presidential elections.

Senator FLAKE. Great. Back to the security environment, the raid that occurred last weekend, nobody faults—I guess it was not successful. We did not get our target there, and I am sure the commanders made the right decision. But how does that affect our policy going forward? What challenges does that present to us to have another failed raid into the country? Does that embolden al-Shabaab, or what happens, Ms. Dory, moving ahead?

Ms. DORY. From my perspective, taking direct action is one element of the multifaceted approach being taken vis-a-vis al-Shabaab and the circumstances under which that is pursued were outlined by the President in his National Defense University speech. There are selected cases where that will be pursued.

More importantly, though, is the indirect approach and the three major pieces of that. We have talked about two of them in particular. One is continuing to support AMISOM and its activities against al-Shabaab. The second is working with Somali National Security Services and their ability to develop an effective counterterrorism capability going forward. And the third that we have not really touched on yet is the work that we are doing with the other partners in the region on a bilateral basis, whether it is directly with the Kenyans, directly with the Ethiopians, Djibouti, and Uganda. All of them have faced various threats from al-Shabaab based on their willingness to participate in AMISOM. Several of those have borne the results in terms of attacks in their territory. And a key part of the strategy vis-a-vis al-Shabaab is also the continued support to those bilateral partners in the region.

Senator FLAKE. Thank you, Mr. Chairman.

Senator COONS. Thank you.

Senator McCain.

Senator McCAIN. Thank you, Mr. Chairman.

I thank the witnesses.

Ms. Dory, the operation in Somalia—it is my understanding from published reports that they did not go forward with the mission because there was greater resistance than they had anticipated. Is that an accurate media depiction of what happened?

Ms. DORY. Senator, I think to discuss the operational details; we would have to move into a different setting.

Senator McCAIN. Well, could you say whether the media reporting was accurate or inaccurate?

Ms. DORY. I think to get into the operational details that would confirm or not confirm the media reporting would require us to move into a different setting.

Senator McCAIN. So I guess what you are saying is that we have to have information in a secure setting, but it is OK if the media report events and yet you can neither corroborate nor deny those events. Is that correct?

Ms. DORY. That is correct in this setting.

Senator MCCAIN. Well, do not be surprised, Ms. Dory, when there is skepticism here about the activities that you engage in. The fact is it was a failure. The fact is that there was an intelligence failure there, otherwise the mission would have been completed. And I guess maybe in another setting, maybe in the New York Times or the Washington Post, we will find out exactly why it failed.

Ms. Dory, given last weekend's operation was justified under the AUMF which, we understand from his State of the Union speech, President Obama seeks to repeal, how will terrorist groups like al-Shabaab be targeted and will these types of operations be justified in the future, absent an AUMF?

Ms. DORY. Senator, I believe going back to the earlier discussion about the direct and indirect approach, at the present time Authorization for Use of Military Force—AUMF—remains in force and is legally available for the direct approach, and the corollary to that is enabling the regional partners, whether it is the Somalis directly, whether it is the regional players who are willing to participate in AMISOM as troop-contributing countries, or others on a bilateral basis, that that will continue to be a core element of the strategy in terms of countering the activities and disrupting al-Shabaab.

Senator MCCAIN. Absent an AUMF, would this operation have been legal?

Ms. DORY. Senator, I am not prepared with the legal analysis for you today, but I can come back to you with a response on that.

[The following information for the record from the Department of Defense to the above question follows:]

Absent the 2001 AUMF, the President always reserves the right under constitutional authority to order certain types of military action in the interest of national security. For example, U.S. Armed Forces took limited forcible action against elements of al-Qaeda in the 1990s, prior to the enactment of the AUMF. Accordingly, without the current express statutory authorization, the recent counterterrorism operation in Somalia would have been permissible.

Senator MCCAIN. Is it your opinion as to whether it would be legal absent an AUMF?

Ms. DORY. I do not have an independent personal opinion to complement the legal analysis at this point.

Senator MCCAIN. Ms. Linda Thomas-Greenfield, in Somalia it is my understanding that most of the work is being done by private contractors. Is that true?

Ms. THOMAS-GREENFIELD. We do have private contractors assisting us in Somalia, but we are using a mixture of that, as well as direct support to our AMISOM and other strategic partners such as the Ethiopians, and we also work very, very closely with AFRICOM and have some AFRICOM support there.

Senator MCCAIN. Does that mean you have American troops in Somalia?

Ms. THOMAS-GREENFIELD. No, sir. We do not have troops, but we do have an advisor working with the Somalia Government and we do work with the Somali national military outside of Somalia doing training, and we also occasionally send people in to do training with them.

Senator MCCAIN. How do you maintain oversight of what these contractors are doing if there is no American military there?

Ms. THOMAS-GREENFIELD. We do send people in on a regular basis to monitor when we are able to travel, when security allows us to travel inside. And that is part of the issue that we have, that we are not able to travel on a regular basis, but when we are able to travel, we are able to do that kind of monitoring. And we also work and monitor them through our operations in Nairobi.

Senator MCCAIN. These contractors are often operating in what is effectively a combat zone. Would you agree?

Ms. THOMAS-GREENFIELD. Occasionally it is a combat zone.

Senator MCCAIN. You spoke about the goal of normalizing our military-to-military relationship with Somalia. Could you describe what that would look like?

Ms. THOMAS-GREENFIELD. What I would hope for—and it was DDAS Dory who talked about the military-to-military relationship. It is my hope that once the security situation there is enabling, that we would have our military doing regular programs through the same kinds of programs that we do elsewhere in Africa that provide direct training and support to the Somali military. One of our primary goals is to build a professional army there that is able to provide security and is professional and has capacity to respond to al-Shabaab.

Senator MCCAIN. On what grounds did we decide to send contractors in as opposed to our military in? Was it the threat? Was it contractors do a better job? What guided that decision?

Ms. THOMAS-GREENFIELD. We do a mix. We have always had contractors who have supported our efforts, but in some places we do have military. So it was not a decision that we would only use contractors. I think contractors were simpler for us to use on this occasion, but at a point when the security situation changes, we certainly would look at other options.

Senator MCCAIN. So it was based on the security situation.

Ms. THOMAS-GREENFIELD. I think that was part of the issue.

Senator MCCAIN. Well, if it is the security situation that would guide your decision whether to send them in, I would imagine it was the security situation that led you to keep them out.

I thank the witnesses.

Senator COONS. Thank you.

As the Senator referenced and as a number of us have discussed, there have been developments in the region, both in Kenya and Somalia that I think called for a classified briefing, particularly on the Westgate attack in Nairobi and some of the intelligence gathered from there and the regional implications, as well as recent developments in Somalia. And I would welcome the opportunity to discuss the timing in which that might be possible.

Senator MCCAIN. Could I just say I am sure the chairman understands the frustration when we read things in the media that are believed to be factual and we cannot find out in open session whether it is true or not. I think the American people probably deserve to know if it is carried in the media.

Senator COONS. I suspect we broadly share frustration about many of the things we read in the media, not all of which I believe. But I do think at the outset of the hearing I expressed my gratitude to the witnesses for their ability to come today given the impact of the shutdown on departmental resources, legal advice, preparation, and otherwise. And I do think it is appropriate for us to continue some of this line of dialogue in a classified setting, if we could, as soon as possible.

If I might, Assistant Administrator Lindborg, I would be interested. USAID has run programming designed to counter violent extremism and jihadist tendencies within Somalia. Could you say something about the small scale or local or quick impact projects that I believe have been sort of the exemplar of this sort of ongoing effort in the areas that have been secured through AMISOM efforts to try and stabilize the situation and then lay the groundwork for more long-term development work?

Ms. LINDBORG. Yes. You characterized that exactly right. There is an opportunity to show quick wins to some of the communities where you have initial greater security and work with them so those communities identify what are their priorities and coinvest with them in a way that enables local governance structures to have greater credibility with their communities and to align that then with the central approach as it evolves and address essential services, things like additional schools, basic infrastructure.

At the same time, we are very focused on what is a large youth population to provide alternatives to extremism and through our Somali youth initiative working to both provide secondary education opportunities, as well as economic options and ways for them to participate in civic life. We think this is absolutely critical especially for those groups.

And with your permission, I also wanted to just clarify Senator Flake's question about the democratic election of the President and the assembly. The constituent assembly was formed and they then elected the President. Somalia is not currently able to have the kind of representative elections that we think about in this country. That is a part of the big effort over the next several years, is to provide that kind of election commission and voter registration that they are simply not equipped to do right now. So there is a difference between democratically elected and elected through representative voting that I wanted to just use the moment to clarify.

Senator FLAKE. Yes. I just was taken a bit aback when you said ''democratically elected'' earlier on. It is more like selected. And I agree we are not at a point where we can expect anything else, but we cannot lead people to believe that we have a democratically elected government there.

Ms. LINDBORG. It was not a full every voter through the country but a cross section in this constituent assembly which did provide a legitimate government to enable us through this important period at the same time that we are working at the community level to enable those gains to be realized.

Senator COONS. And the overarching goal of the 2016 process is to ultimately get to a place where a legitimate national election is possible.

Ms. LINDBORG. That is right.

Senator COONS. Universal suffrage.

Ms. LINDBORG. Absolutely, with a constitution. And so it is also the process of drafting the constitution and enabling a process of reconciliation and a more inclusive dialogue including, by the way, the diaspora, which is an important player in all of this.

Senator COONS. A steady transition from 20 years of statelessness, lawlessness, and violence to a functioning democracy is part of the objective of this hearing is to understand how best we can support that work.

You have just come back from the new deal conference. I would be interested in hearing in a little more detail how the international community is coordinating its support for this ongoing transition in Somalia and what you see as our role and the international community's role in how well coordinated it is toward the goals we have been discussing.

Ms. LINDBORG. I think this is an essential opportunity because it enables the international donor community to come together in a more coordinated way and to support a plan and a framework that is owned by the Somalis with the key priorities that were laid out. We are able to work together against those priorities, and there are conversations, very vigorous conversations, with the U.K., with Sweden, and our other development partners on how to ensure that our support equals and aligns behind the key priorities.

There is also a timing urgency here, that it is in these moments where there is this rush of confidence and the sense of possibility that we step forward in a coherent manner that moves us forward against a very ambitious timetable. So it is important to grasp, as they call this, ''the golden hour'' of possibility and enable that confidence to turn into real results.

Senator COONS. Thank you.

Madam Assistant Secretary, if I might, what is our overall strategy—help me better understand it—to simultaneously strengthen ongoing Somali-led efforts to develop centralized state institutions and a coordinate federal system given clan-based power centers and some recent ad hoc efforts to form federal states such as Jubaland. My impression from your opening testimony is you think there is steady progress toward both, but there is some tension between whether there is a centralized strong state or a really federalized structure. What do you see as our strategy and the path forward in this particular part of the process?

Ms. THOMAS-GREENFIELD. Our primary goal is that there will be a strong federal framework that will allow the various components and various groups outside the central government to participate in a process of governing the entire country of Somalia. We do need a central government that can provide services, that can lead, that can develop the policies and strategies going forward, but that government has to recognize the components outside of the central government. So we have encouraged cooperation and implementation of the federal framework. We have encouraged the government to be in close coordination and cooperation with Somaliland. We were very supportive of the Jubaland agreement, and we are encouraging further agreements along those lines. The President of Somalia has expressed his views that he is prepared to move forward in that direction, and we are backing him in those efforts.

Senator COONS. Terrific. Thank you very much.

Senator Flake.

Senator FLAKE. Ms. Thomas-Greenfield, you mentioned $140 million going to, I think you said, economic growth activities and democracy activities. Can you further detail where that is going and who is administering that? I think you mentioned the figure $140 million. Right?

Ms. THOMAS-GREENFIELD. That's correct. AID Assistant Administrator Lindborg will address those details. Some $170 million is going to our efforts to support the capacity of the Somali National Army and supporting training for that, but we also are building democratic institutions that are being worked with USAID.

Senator FLAKE. OK. Can you further detail the democracy activities or economic growth activities that we are involved in?

Ms. LINDBORG. Sure. We have about a $64 million program for 2011 and 2012—sorry—2012 and 2013 that is working to—some of the activities that I already detailed to help set up the constitution, to support the move toward elections. That also includes work in Somaliland and Puntland with those governments to continue to support the very important advances they have already made on democratic approaches, transparency, accountability, and to align their policies with the federal government and includes a lot of the work on setting up the independent election commission and the electoral law, the mechanics, to make the gains that we need in the next 36 months.

Senator FLAKE. Turning to Somaliland and Puntland, you kind of make it sound as if they are okay with this arrangement, and that is not the sense I have received from them. They want to be recognized on their own. Can you kind of explain the difference here?

Ms. THOMAS-GREENFIELD. Yes, and that is the sense we have gotten as well, that they have worked to develop and stabilize the areas that are under their control, but we are following in the lead of the AU. We have not recognized them as separate governments at this time because the AU has not made that recognition. But we continue to support their efforts to provide security and services to the people that they are currently supporting.

Senator FLAKE. You mentioned some of the funding is actually going to Somaliland and Puntland to help them. What is their understanding as to what they are to do with this money? Are they establishing their place in a federal system? Because it sounds to me, when you talk to them, that they have a completely different idea of where they are going. What is your understanding, Ms. Lindborg?

Ms. LINDBORG. As I indicated, there is continued help particularly to support the accountability and transparency that they quite appropriately have already made gains with, and at the same time, we are doing it in a way that very expressly indicates the goal of having that align with the central government in a centrally federated system.

Senator FLAKE. And they accept that?

Ms. LINDBORG. There are conversations ongoing.

Senator FLAKE. All right. Just kind of a general observation and I will go ahead and stop. But we all know this is tough work. This is a tough environment. You know, where you had basically a lawless situation with no central government for 20 years, nobody can expect it to immediately transform into some flourishing democracy. We understand that. But I get the sense from the testimony that you are painting a little rosier picture than actually exists there, and I am not sure that that does us any good as those who have to authorize and appropriate money to sustain programs. And I will be interested in the next panel to see their thoughts on that.

But just to let you know, we recognize this is tough and it is going to be a rocky road, but it does not do us any good to gloss over difficulties. And my suspicion is that, you know, the government—they are trying. We want them to succeed. We recognize them. But there are likely large swaths of the country that do not recognize the government as legitimate, and we need to recognize that and move forward. But it is a tough road. I know we are doing the best we can, but it is likely a more difficult situation than perhaps we are told.

But I thank you.

Senator COONS. Thank you, Senator Flake.

Senator McCain.

Senator MCCAIN. No more questions.

Senator COONS. For this panel then, if I might—we do have a whole other panel, and we hope to come to some conclusion of this hearing. I want to thank you for your testimony and for your very hard work. There has been significant progress made in Somalia relative to where it was 2 years ago, a lawless state characterized by widespread piracy, humanitarian crises, and the utter absence of a functioning federal government. So to Senator Flake's point, great progress has been made, but significant hurdles and challenges remain, as I believe you have been clear. And I look forward to working with you closely as we articulate together a coherent U.S. strategy moving forward to take advantage of this moment and this opportunity.

Thank you.

And I would like to invite our second panel to take their places in front of the committee.

[Pause.]

Senator COONS. I would like to welcome our second panel today: first, Andre Le Sage, senior research fellow at the National Defense University's Institute for Strategic Studies; Abdi Aynte, founder of the Heritage Institute for Policy Studies in Mogadishu; and E.J. Hogendoorn, deputy director for Africa at the International Crisis Group. And I would like to invite each of you in turn to make your opening statement, if you might, to the committee.

Dr. Le Sage.

STATEMENT OF DR. ANDRE LE SAGE, SENIOR RESEARCH FELLOW FOR AFRICA, INSTITUTE FOR NATIONAL STRATEGIC STUDIES, NATIONAL DEFENSE UNIVERSITY, WASHINGTON, DC

Dr. LE SAGE. Thank you, Senator Coons, Senator Flake, and members of the subcommittee. It is an honor to appear before you today.

As requested in your invitation, I will focus my remarks on the status of al-Shabaab and international efforts to defeat that terrorist group. I would be grateful if my full written statement could be included in the record.

Senator COONS. Without objection.

Dr. LE SAGE. Al-Shabaab has been weakened as a national insurgency force. However, it retains the capability to conduct targeted guerilla and terrorist attacks against Somali, United States, and partner nation interests. This was vividly demonstrated in September when al-Shabaab-linked gunmen stormed the Westgate shopping complex in Nairobi killing scores of innocent civilians. Without additional efforts to defeat al-Shabaab, it is only a matter of time before the group and its affiliates undertake additional deadly attacks.

Al-Shabaab, currently led by the group's emir, Ahmed Abdi Godane, has controlled much of south-central Somalia since 2006. However, over the past 2 years, the tide has turned dramatically. AMISOM has partnered with former clan militia that have integrated into the Somali National Army. They pressured al-Shabaab to withdraw from Mogadishu in August 2011 and then seized neighboring towns. In 2012, Ethiopia and Kenya also worked with clan militia to liberate the towns of Baidoa and Kismayo. In central Somalia and Puntland, clan leaders and local administrations have also mobilized to resist the al-Shabaab movement.

In response to the military superiority of AMISOM in Ethiopia, al-Shabaab has avoided conventional engagements. Instead the group has shifted its forces to safe havens that lie just outside of AMISOM's reach. Examples include Barawe in Lower Shabelle, Bulo Burti in Hiran region, and the Golis Mountains in Puntland. From these locations, al-Shabaab employs its intelligence wing, the Amniyat, to launch hit-and-run attacks and place IED's and carry out assassinations and suicide bombings. The Amniyat, led my Mahad Karate, is comprised of hard-liners loyal to Godane.

At the same time, al-Shabaab's regional governors are essential components of its network. They maintain al-Shabaab's control over local populations, allow terrorist training camps to operate, raise funds through taxes and extortion, conduct recruitment, and manage clan relations.

As the Westgate attack shows, al-Shabaab also retains a significant external operations capability. These individuals, including both Somalis and foreign fighters, are only loosely under Godane's control. They are dedicated to exporting terrorism across East Africa and work closely with affiliates such as al-Hijra in Kenya and the Ansar Muslim Youth Centre in Tanzania.

Since becoming the group's emir, Godane has personalized command and control and marginalized senior al-Shabaab leaders who disagree with his decisions. Long-standing tensions between Godane and his deputy, Mukhtar Robow, broke into open violence in June 2013. Many analysts hoped this internal conflict would weaken al-Shabaab. However, this is not the case. For several years, Godane has been building a splinter faction primarily based around the Amniyat and has taken control of the group's funding and operational planning.

Al-Shabaab's long-term strategy does remain a matter of debate. The group may be playing a waiting game, retreating from large battles to preserve its strength and using terrorist attacks to stay relevant for as long as possible in hopes that the wider political context in Somalia and East Africa will change, allowing al-Shabaab to resurge. This would be the case if the Somali Government fails, if al-Shabaab can align with clan-based opposition groups, or if new regional crises force AMISOM troop-contributing countries to depart Somalia.

Godane and his hard-line supporters have no allusions that they can impose an extremist state on Somalia if AMISOM and regional forces continue to make the progress they have done and the Somali Federal Government works to stabilize the area. In this case, the group may be satisfied managing a clandestine jihadist struggle that commits nihilistic acts of violence for as long as possible.

To conclude, although al-Shabaab has, indeed, lost control of key cities in Somalia, the group has recalibrated its approach and remains a vicious enemy. The United States and its Somali and international partners need to redouble efforts to roll back the group while supporting Somalia's Federal Government to consolidate security gains. This requires a combination of efforts.

First, we must revive the regional offensive against al-Shabaab, including increased operational and intelligence support for both AMISOM and Ethiopia.

Second, it is critical to develop a capable and professional national security structure in Somalia that can fight side by side with its regional partners.

Third, additional diplomacy and foreign aid are needed to support the Somali Federal Government and the local administrations with which it is working to oppose al-Shabaab and to build a federal structure. They need to negotiate power and resource-sharing deals that allow the country's federal structure to function.

Finally, we must continue supporting Somalia's neighbors, particularly Kenya where the Westgate attacks took place, but also Tanzania and other countries that serve as hosts to al-Shabaab-affiliated movements in the region.

Mr. Chairman, thank you again for the opportunity to testify, and I look forward to your questions.

[The prepared statement of Dr. Le Sage follows:]

PREPARED STATEMENT OF DR. ANDRE LE SAGE

Thank you and good afternoon, Mr. Chairman, Mr. Ranking Member, and members of the subcommittee. It is an honor to appear before you today to discuss Somalia's ongoing political and security transition, and the ways in which the United States can promote stability and combat terrorism in East Africa.

Mr. Chairman, as requested in your letter of invitation, I will focus my remarks on the status of al-Shabaab in Somalia, and the progress of international efforts to defeat that terrorist group. Before I begin, let me note that my comments reflect my personal analysis, not the positions of U.S. policy or the National Defense University (NDU).

My overall assessment is that al-Shabaab has indeed been weakened as a conventional insurgency force. However, it retains the capability and intent to employ guerilla and terrorist attacks that inflict deadly harm against U.S. and partner-nation interests both inside Somalia and across the region. This was vividly demonstrated on September 21, when al-Shabaab-linked terrorists stormed the Westgate shopping complex in Nairobi, Kenya, killing scores of innocent civilians—including Africans and non-Africans; Muslims and non-Muslims; men, women and children.

Without additional efforts to defeat the group, it is only a matter of time before al-Shabaab undertakes additional deadly attacks. Moreover, there is a significant danger that al-Shabaab's brutal tactics will set a precedent for other al-Qaeda-affiliates and "lone wolf" terrorists that are intent on doing harm to the United States and its allies.

THE POLITICAL & SECURITY CONTEXT

Al-Shabaab—which is currently led by the group's emir, Ahmed Abdi "Godane"—was established by 2004 by a small group of Somali Islamist militants. They had been part of an earlier Islamist movement—Al Itihad al Islamia (AIAI)—and had provided protection and support for the Al Qaeda East Africa (AQEA) cell that was responsible for the 1998 attacks on the U.S. Embassies in Kenya and Tanzania. As of 2004, al-Shabaab operatives were functioning independently from AIAI, conducting assassinations of Somali peace activists and security officials, as well as foreign journalists and aid workers.

Al-Shabaab's existence became publicly known in 2006 when it served as a self-appointed vanguard force within the Union of Islamic Courts (UIC). The UIC took control of much of southern Somalia after it defeated the clan-based warlords that had dominated southern Somalia since the fall of the Siad Barre regime in 1991. Ethiopian military intervention in Somalia from 2007–2009 defeated the UIC, and installed the Transitional Federal Government (TFG) and African Union (AU) peacekeepers in Mogadishu.

While the TFG languished amidst political infighting, al-Shabaab successfully launched an insurgency campaign that gradually retook control of southern Somalia. Moreover, al-Shabaab increasingly gained control over all foreign fighters in Somalia, including those loyal to AQEA. This was a byproduct of the success of international security operations targeting senior AQEA operatives Saleh Ali Saleh "Nabhan," Fazul Abdullah Mohamed "Harun" and others. As a result, the al-Shabaab movement today combines the traits of a local insurgency seeking to impose an extremist Islamic state on Somalia, and the traits of a transnational terrorist group that seeks to conduct attacks outside of Somalia's borders in the name of global jihad.

In 2011, the tide began to turn dramatically against al-Shabaab. The African Union Mission to Somalia (AMISOM) partnered with former clan-based militia in Mogadishu that had been integrated into a nominal Somali National Army (SNA). They succeeded in pressuring al-Shabaab to execute a "tactical withdrawal" from Mogadishu in August 2011, and subsequently liberated several key towns in Lower and Middle Shabelle regions from al-Shabaab control (including Afgooye, Merka, Jowhar, Wanleweyn and others). Combined ground offensives by Ethiopian and Kenyan militaries then succeeded in wresting control of those countries' border regions from al-Shabaab, and liberated the major cities of Baidoa and Kismayo in 2012. Finally, in Central Somalia, Ethiopia supported clan leaders and the Sufist movement Ahlu Sunna wal Jama'a (ASWJ) to create local administrations that could resist al-Shabaab's presence.

SOMALIA'S FEDERAL GOVERNMENT

As al-Shabaab lost ground, there was a general assumption that the movement was significantly weakened and could be defeated by (1) the gradual expansion of AMISOM's area of control, and (2) efforts to build a post-transitional national government. Global attention slowly shifted away from security issues to Somalia's political scene with the establishment of Somalia's Federal Government (SFG) in September 2012.

The SFG—led by President Hassan Sheikh Mohamud, Speaker of Parliament Mohamed Osman Jawari, and other Somali intellectuals with longstanding civil society ties—has received remarkable levels of international support. This includes inter alia the formal recognition of the Federal Government by dozens of countries around the world and the reestablishment of traditional diplomatic ties; increased foreign aid from the United States and other major donors; the partial lifting of the international arms embargo on Somalia; negotiations with the World Bank and International Monetary Fund to reestablish formal relations; and efforts by the United Nations to shift from Kenya-based, cross-border to in-country operations.

The leadership of the SFG will be critical to completing Somalia's transitional process, and they will require substantial international diplomatic, military and financial support in the process. At the same time, it is important to understand that much of Somalia's political and security progress over the past few years has been the result of a combination of factors:

1. Somalia's warlords and militia-factions, which dominated the country's political, economic, and security affairs since 1991, were disarmed by the Union of Islamic Courts (UIC) in 2006. Since then, the warlords have not been able to rebuild their powerbase and no longer exercise a veto on Somalia's progress.

2. At the same time, popular support for al-Shabaab has dwindled quickly. When it controlled most of southern Somalia, the group failed to govern effectively. It dispensed with international aid agencies amidst famine conditions, levied high taxes and forced conscription to support the group's war effort, and imposed extremely severe forms of shari'a law. As a result, Somalis had little interest in continuing to support the group, while more moderate Islamist movements splintered away.

3. Many major clans—whose warlords had been disarmed by al-Shabaab—have worked to reestablish their political position and began to resist the movement. This includes major segments of the Marehan and Ogaden in Gedo Region, former supporters of the Rahanweyn Resistance Army (RRA) in Bay and Bakol Regions, the Hawadle in Hiraan, and the Habr Gedir who supported formation of the Sufist movement Ahlu Sunna wal Jama'a (ASWJ) movement, Galmudug State and Himan and Heeb State. With assistance from Ethiopia and Kenya, these groups began to create local administrations and participate in anti-Shabaab military activities.

4. AMISOM is an overwhelming military force relative to both al-Shabaab and any clan-based forces that may oppose its mandate. AMISOM now requires additional forces and enablers (including helicopters) to continue their advance, but thus far have been able to roll back al-Shabaab and hold locations that they ''liberate.''

5. Many of Somalia's militia are slowly integrating into battalions and brigades that form the nucleus of the Somali National Army (SNA) in Mogadishu. Outside the capital city, militia that were initially proxy forces for Ethiopia or Kenya may now be incorporated into a national command-and-control structure. All of this is supported by Western aid that provides salaries, training, equipment and mentors to professionalize the SNA—much of which has been funded by the United States.

6. Finally, regional politics across the Horn of Africa have begun working in Somalia's favor. In particular, Ethiopia is now working to support the SFG, including brokering the recent Addis Ababa agreement to form the Interim Jubba Administration. At the same time, countries such as Eritrea—which previously supported spoilers of Somalia's peace process—are no longer significantly active in the country.

In addition to supporting the SFG, defeating al-Shabaab and building a sustainable post-transition government for Somalia will require national, regional, and international efforts to sustain these trends.

THE CURRENT AL-SHABAAB THREAT NETWORK

Despite these positive political developments, al-Shabaab remains a determined and vicious enemy. To conserve its forces and resources, al-Shabaab has avoided direct, conventional engagements with AMISOM, the Ethiopian military and the emerging SNA forces. Instead, al-Shabaab has withdrawn from their areas of advance and shifted its forces and focus in several directions to establish new safe haven areas, including:

- *Southwest Somalia Safe Haven:* A zone in the far southwest of Somalia that lays between the villages of Barawe in Lower Shabelle, Jilib in Lower Juba, Bardhere in southern Gedo, and Dinsoor in Bay region.
- *Central Somalia Safe Haven:* A zone in the central regions north of Mogadishu, based in Bulo Burti village of southern Hiran region and extending west in Bakol region, east to the towns El Bur and El Dheer in Galgadud, and south into rural areas of Middle Shabelle.
- *Golis Mountains Safe Haven:* A small, mountainous zone outside Bosasso city in the northeastern region of Puntland, running from Galgala toward Badhan, and affording al-Shabaab with the potential to attack key Puntland cities including Bosasso, Garowe and Galkayo.
    - *Somaliland Safe Haven:* The northwestern area of Somaliland, al-Shabaab likely retains a limited capacity to operate. While al-Shabaab has no standing military capacity in this region, it does maintain a clandestine network capable of terrorist attacks, and a network of facilitators that support recruitment, indoctrination, training, weapons trafficking and support for the movement of men and materiel.

In these safe havens, al-Shabaab's regional governors and ideologues are essential components of the network. They maintain al-Shabaab's local control, allow for terrorist training camps to operate, raise funds from taxes and extorting the local community, and manage clan relations and recruitment. Their ranks include well-known al-Shabaab leaders—such as Yassin Kilwe and Abdulkadir Mumin in Puntland; Hassan Yakub and Hassan Fidow in Central Somalia; Yusuf Kabakutukade in Middle Shabelle; Moalim Jinow in Bay and Bakol Regions; and Abdirahman Fidow and Mohamed Dulyadeen in the Juba Valley area. However, despite their critical role in the group's hierarchy, these leaders do not appear to be the focus not a focus of counterterrorism efforts.

Al-Shabaab employs its intelligence wing, the Amniyat, to infiltrate SFG- and AMISOM-held cities and to emplace improvised explosive devices (IEDs), conduct assassinations or carry out suicide bombing attacks. This group, led by Mahad Mohamed Ali "Karate," is comprised of hard-liners loyal to al-Shabaab's emir Godane and serves as the movement's parallel governance structure to monitor and regulate the actions of other leaders who may be opposed to Godane. In addition, al-Shabaab's guerilla militias are used primarily for hit-and-run attacks against AMISOM and SNA forward operating bases and main supply routes.

Finally, as demonstrated by the Westgate mall attack last month, al-Shabaab retains a significant "external operations" cadre, existing either within or distinct from the Amniyat unit. These individuals, including both Somalis and foreign fighters, are dedicated to expanding the reach of al-Shabaab and the wider al-Qaeda network to conduct terrorist operations outside of Somalia. The region has a long history of terrorist attacks, including the 1998 bombings of the U.S. Embassies in Nairobi and Dar es Salaam, the 2002 attacks targeting tourists in Mombasa, and the 2010 Kampala attacks the end of the 2010 FIFA World Cup. As al-Shabaab has lost ground in Somalia, more of its trained and battle-hardened fighters have focused on other parts of East Africa, particularly through cooperation with local affiliates such as Al Hijra in Kenya, and the Ansar Muslim Youth Centre (A–MYC) in Tanzania.

SUSTAINING AL-SHABAAB: FUNDING AND PERSONNEL

Al-Shabaab's finances have been dramatically reduced as a result of its loss of safe haven to the military offensives undertaken by AMISOM, regional partners and the SFG. Prior to those offensives, Kismayo seaport—from which charcoal and other commodities were traded—provided al-Shabaab with its primary source of revenue. Nonetheless, al-Shabaab is still able to access funds and manage their distribution across its areas of operations in order to sustain its personnel and undertake guerilla attacks. In particular, al-Shabaab continues to levy taxes on national and regional trade routes that cross al-Shabaab safe haven areas. The group extorts revenue from major businesses under threat of attack and coerces donations in cash or in kind from clan-based communities in areas that it controls. Finally, al-Shabaab likely still receives foreign donations by supporters of its jihadi ideology.

Al-Shabaab today has a reduced number of personnel as the result of two factors: first, the growing resistance of major Somali subclans, and second, the successful military offensives by AMISOM, regional partners and the SFG. As a result, many clan-based militia who joined al-Shabaab when the movement occupied their traditional clan areas or who supported al-Shabaab in order to gain financial payments have left the movement. The reduction in the number of clan-based personnel supporting al-Shabaab is a positive factor in so far as the reduction degrades the fighting capabilities of the movement. However, a smaller, more ideologically committed force is easier to sustain for al-Shabaab's leadership, particularly given the group's potentially declining access to funds.

Nonetheless, al-Shabaab has demonstrated its capacity to sustain thousands of personnel in its safe haven areas, and remains able to surge militia in the hundreds against specific targets, particularly in rural areas of south-central Somalia. In addition, some Somali sub-clans—for example, the Duduble and Murosade in Mogadishu and Central Somalia, or the Warsangeli and Lelkase in Puntland—have aligned themselves with al-Shabaab in order to strengthen their lineages' hand in longstanding struggles against other subclans for local political and economic control. This affords al-Shabaab a continued supply of militia recruits and funding, as well as safe haven and safe passage.

AL-SHABAAB'S INTERNAL CONFLICTS

Since its creation, al-Shabaab was nominally led through the collective decision-making of its Shura Council. However, following the appointment of Godane as the group's emir, he has personalized command-and-control, marginalized other senior al-Shabaab leaders who disagree with his decisions, and even arrested or killed Somali and foreign fighters who seek to develop their own operational plans.

Longstanding leadership tensions between al-Shabaab's emir Godane and his deputy, Mukhtar Robow, broke into open violence in June 2013. Forces loyal to Godane killed several key leaders, including Godane's mentor, Ibrahim Haji Jama "al-Afghani." Following the fighting, Robow has sought protection in his clan's home on the border between Bay and Bakol regions. Meanwhile, the U.S. jihadist Omar Hammami "Abu Mansor al-Amriki" was killed by Godane's faction, Hassan Dahir Aweis (one of the original AIAI leaders from the 1990s) fled and was arrested by the SFG, and other senior leaders expect they may be next.

Many analysts and policymakers hoped this internal conflict would weaken al-Shabaab and make it less capable to launch attacks. However, that is obviously not the case. For several years, Godane had been building and taking firm control over a splinter faction of al-Shabaab—primarily based around the Amniyat intelligence unit—and he has centralized control over the al-Shabaab movement, including its forces, funding and operational planning.

It is worth noting that the Amniyat, which leads attacks against Somali and AMISOM forces in Mogadishu, was barely impacted when the infighting broke out this past summer. Their attack rate in Mogadishu never fell, and the severity of those attacks never dulled. Over the past year, they have also succeeded in conducting several major attacks including those against senior SFG officials, the Turkish Embassy, the United Nations compound, as well as popular restaurants and hotels.

AL-SHABAAB'S STRATEGY AND THE WESTGATE ATTACK

Al-Shabaab's long-term strategy is not entirely clear. On the one hand, the group may be playing a "waiting game." By this analysis, al-Shabaab is working hard to stay alive, to preserve its strength and to stay relevant for as long as possible. It hopes that the wider political context in Somalia and the region will change and al-Shabaab will have an opportunity to resurge. This would be the case if the SFG fails to rebuild a national government, if new clan-based opposition groups emerge with which al-Shabaab can align its movement, or if new regional crises force AMISOM to depart Somalia.

On the other hand, Godane, his loyal Amniyat structure, and his external operations cadre may have no illusions that they will eventually succeed in imposing an extremist Islamic state on Somalia. By this account, the group is satisfied with managing a clandestine jihadist movement that inflicts serious harm through nihilistic violence for as long as possible.

In this context, the attack on the Westgate shopping mall in Nairobi should not come as a surprise. Al-Shabaab and its regional networks across East Africa have long harbored both the ambition and capability to conduct such a deadly attack. Nonetheless, the attack begs a series of questions regarding the level of external threat posed by al-Shabaab.

There should be no doubt that al-Shabaab's emir and spokesman both claimed credit for the attack, and have threatened additional bloodshed. Almost certainly, the Westgate attack was a combined operation involving an element of the al-Shabaab network in Somalia, and an element of the its Kenyan affiliate, the Al Hijra network. From an intelligence perspective, the key is to identify exactly which individuals were involved and their chain of command. Was the attack authorized and directed by Godane to demonstrate that he is now fully in charge of the al-Shabaab movement and indispensable to al-Qaeda's senior leaders despite his group's recent infighting? Or, was the attack planned and undertaken by remnants of the AQEA network and foreign fighters that have felt undermined by Godane—acting independently and forcing al-Shabaab leadership to catch up?

It will also be critical to assess what form of "intelligence failure" allowed the Westgate attack to happen. In short, we need to understand why the attack cell was not identified in advance. How long was the attack cell in Kenya before they took action? Was the attack cell "too quick" from its infiltration into Kenya until the execution of their plot for local security service (even with foreign assistance) to take action? Was the attack cell in Kenya for a long time and parts of previously identified, but considered a "watch target" by mistake? Or, was the attack cell not identified at all due to sufficient compartmentalization and operational security?

The challenge in answering these questions today is the huge amount of contradictory information that exists in the public domain, and the possibility of developing reasonable hypotheses to support many different assessments. Answers to these questions will eventually emerge as the investigation moves forward. In the meantime, it is critical to focus on the best possible response to prevent such an attack from happening again.

CONTINUING THE FIGHT AGAINST AL-SHABAAB

As detailed above, al-Shabaab has indeed been weakened as a conventional insurgency force inside Somalia. However, the group has recalibrated its approach and retains the capability and intent to employ guerilla and terrorist attacks. In response, the United States and its Somali, regional and international partners need to redouble their efforts to roll back al-Shabaab and build a national, federal government for Somalia that can consolidate the country's security gains into the future.

Succeeding to defeat the al-Shabaab insurgency and prevent the resurgence of al-Qaeda-inspired terrorist cells across East Africa will require a combination of efforts:

- Reviving Regionally-Supported Offensive Operations against al-Shabaab:

  Æ Increase intelligence collection and sharing, as well as operational support, for regional security partners to support targeted operations that remove key al-Shabaab and other al-Qaeda-linked operatives from Somalia, and disrupt terrorist training camps.

  Æ Strengthen regional military commitments to sustain and increase the capabilities of AMISOM and their ability to work alongside the SFG's security structure and regional partners, including Ethiopia.

  Æ Invest in the development of a capable and professional national security structure in Somalia, including the Somali National Army (SNA), the National Intelligence and Security Agency (NISA) and the Somali National Police (SNP), including careful attention to the integration of anti-Shabaab forces at the local and regional levels.

- Support for the development of Somalia's federal system:

  Æ Provide diplomatic and foreign aid support to the SFG and its local-level Somali governance partners to achieve negotiated durable political agreements, power-sharing and resource-sharing deals that allow for the emergence of a federal governing system.

  Æ Address the vexing and politically charged question of how ''federalism'' will be implemented, including the need to finalize the Provisional Constitution and to negotiate with both longstanding, quasi-independent administrations in Puntland and Somaliland, and nascent, clan-based administrations formed across south-central Somalia.

  Æ Ensure the continued formation of national security forces that reflect the decentralized, clan-based reality of the country's post-war political economy, which is enshrined in Somalia's new federal structure.

  Æ Support the SFG and its federal units to develop, resource, and implement sectoral strategies and regulatory mechanisms to ensure the delivery of essential public goods, including health care, education and development, as well as training a new civil service cadre after 20 years without a functioning government.

  Æ Support the SFG and its federal units to establish positive control over Somalia's resource flows, including anticorruption efforts and tax revenues from Mogadishu's key economic infrastructure points (airport, seaport, checkpoints, and markets).

- Support for regional partners to combat terrorism:

  Æ Continue support for Kenya, Tanzania, Uganda, Ethiopia and other regional partners who are vulnerable to attacks by al-Shabaab and its regional affiliates, including Al Hijra and the A–MYC.

  Æ Build regional security cooperation between these countries and the SFG to prevent future attacks.

Senator COONS. Thank you very much, Dr. Le Sage, for that testimony. I look forward to the opportunity to ask questions, if I might.

Next, Mr. Aynte.

STATEMENT OF ABDI AYNTE, DIRECTOR, HERITAGE INSTITUTE FOR POLICY STUDIES, MOGADISHU, SOMALIA

Mr. AYNTE. Chairman Coons, Ranking Member Flake, thank you very much for the opportunity to participate in this important panel at this critical juncture in Somalia's history.

One year after the formation of the first nontraditional government in over 20 years, there are reasons to be cautiously optimistic about the future of Somalia. The Somali people are determined more than ever to reclaim their dignity and, above all, their place among the community of nations.

They have also identified a common enemy to peace and stability. Citizens across the country are countering al-Shabaab's destruction and despair with construction and hope. Signs of economic vibrancy are reemerging. The Somali diaspora are returning in large numbers, bringing with them much-needed skills, business opportunities and, most importantly, a sense of normalcy. And this is where the issue of remittance comes in and it is important for the United States to support the flow of remittance to the people of Somalia.

Significant parts of Somalia suggest Somaliland and Puntland and others are also enjoying relative peace, stability, and self-governance.

With regards to security, gains are less encouraging. Despite losing control of most major cities in Somalia, al-Shabaab fighters remain a major threat to peace. The capital of Mogadishu, where I came from just 2 days ago, is under constant assault.

A key challenge to the restoration of stability is the chronic weakness of security apparatuses. Command, control, and coordination is demonstrably weak due to the fragmentation of militias forming the security forces. Training, especially on protection of vulnerable civilians, remains poor and uncoordinated with many countries running various programs. The composition of forces does not reflect the regional and clan diversity of the Somali people, depriving the security forces of a much-needed legitimacy.

The U.S. Government has provided significant support to Somalia's struggling security forces and the African Union peacekeeping missions for many years. This support from the United States and other development partners is literally all that is standing between the collapse of the federal government and its survival.

The U.S. Government must, however, utilize its support innovatively. Tactical counterterrorism measures, surgical strikes, and the provision of ammunition were necessary for some time, but now there is a greater need for strategic partnership. Resources must be channeled toward rebuilding competent, professional, accountable, and broadly representative Somali security services that have both the qualitative and quantitative advantage over the enemy. AMISOM has done an excellent job of recovering regions from al-Shabaab's tyranny, but they cannot become a substitute for indigenous forces. Somali forces can ultimately defeat al-Shabaab.

Security is inextricably linked to political accommodation and reconciliation, which is partially why Somalia adopted a federal model of governance nearly 10 years ago. But a consensus on which type of federalism remains elusive. Successive governments have failed to translate the federal vision into viable member states. Frustrated with the lack of progress at the national level, communities across the country are taking matters into their own hands and are carving out fiefdoms along clan lines. The American dual track policy, which led to direct U.S. engagement with subnational entities, sent the wrong signal that the international community was promoting sectarian polities at the expense of a contiguous federal government.

The process of federating the government faces three enormous challenges.

First, the provisional constitution is deeply ambiguous and contradictory about the shape and the future of the Federal Government of Somalia and divisions of powers between the center and the peripheries. The meaning of federalism broadly misunderstood by the Somali people, many of whom are legitimately nervous about an overly centralized state. This is compounded by the absence of an effective judicial branch that can interpret constitutional provisions.

Second, state institutions that are supposed to play a leading role in the national dialogue and the design of a suitable federal structure are yet to be established. The constitution calls for the formation of nearly a dozen independent commissions, half of which are instrumental to the federation process, such as the Boundaries and Federation Commission, the Inter-State Commission, and the Constitution Review and Implementation Commission. These delays are inexcusable.

The federal government garnered an unprecedented support from the Somali people following its inauguration in September 2012. It also won an unparalleled backing from the international community, including formal recognition by the U.S. Government for the first time in 20 years, easing of the U.N. arms embargo, monthly direct budgetary support from Turkey, and an expanded African Union peacekeeping mission. Many Somalis believe that the federal government has fallen significantly short of using that positive momentum to advance inclusive politics and dialogue with key domestic actors, including existing and emerging federal member states, traditional elders, and civil society.

Third, neighboring countries are sometimes seen as undermining state-building efforts by encouraging and sometimes helping with the formation of more subnational entities to suit their own interests. While Ethiopia and Kenya face real threats from Somalia, as we have seen in the recent appalling attack in Nairobi, their unchecked interference risks destabilizing the country and a reversal of recent fragile gains.

The provisional constitution of Somalia envisions elections to take place toward the end of 2016. While this is not impossible, it is highly improbable, given the magnitude of tasks ahead. It should remain an admirable goal for the current government, but we must not substitute state-building for process-building. Elections are not an end in themselves, but rather a means toward the more vital objective of forming a viable state. That includes finalizing the constitution, settling on a federal structure, and adopting political party laws.

The challenges of facing the process of federation and political consolidation in Somalia are tremendous but not insurmountable.

First, the provisional constitution is a deeply flawed document that contradicts itself and puts future member states and the federal government on a direct collision course. The Somali people and their government need urgent assistance in this regard.

Priority must be given to the formation of the Review and Implementation Commission and Boundaries and Federation Commission. Once established, they will need considerable financial and human resources to engage in genuine national dialogue. There are a number of American institutions with relevant experience that can provide essential support in this area.

Second, assistance to the Somali Government must be contingent upon measurable gains. It must be held accountable to the provisional constitution and its own national plan. If none of the commissions is established by early next year, the Somali people will lose faith in the government's commitment to offer something more than its predecessors.

The United States and its allies should assist the Somali people to develop mechanisms to hold their government accountable. Somali civil society has always been, and will continue to be, a powerful force for progress. The role of civil society is currently worryingly absent. Civil society institutions must be strengthened and given the tools they need to effectively monitor the progress and integrity of the government.

Third, as an important ally to both Kenya and Ethiopia, the United States has a moral obligation to exert pressure on the two countries to allow the Somali people and their government to engage in a national reconciliation. Interference galvanizes militant groups and further divides Somali communities.

The United States should certainly continue to assist both countries in mitigating the security threats they face, but Kenya and Ethiopia must realize that only a democratic, strong, and vibrant Somali state on their borders is the greatest guarantor of security and prosperity in the region.

Mr. Chairman, it is at times easy to dismiss Somalia as being irreparable and the archetypal failed state beyond hope. But as those of us who have given up their comfortable lives and families in the diaspora and returned home can attest to, progress is possible, and it is happening right now.

Somalia has made a profound leap from where it was just 3½ years ago when I first started going back home. At the time, al-Shabaab controlled 75 percent of Mogadishu and almost 60 percent of the entire nation. Pirates were disrupting global shipping lanes. The very notion of government was actually contested across the country.

But with the support of international partners like the United States, the European Union, the African Union, the United Kingdom, and Turkey, and others, Somalia is slowly emerging from the abyss. What it now needs is relentless efforts to rebuild inclusive state institutions that have legitimacy, capacity, and resources needed to finish the mammoth tasks ahead.

I thank you on the subcommittee for this opportunity to present my views and will be happy to answer any questions.

[The prepared statement of Mr. Aynte follows:]

PREPARED STATEMENT OF ABDI AYNTE

Chairman Coons, Ranking Member Flake, subcommittee members, thank you for the opportunity to participate in this important panel at this critical juncture in Somalia's history.

My name is Abdi Aynte, and I am the executive director of the Heritage Institute for Policy Studies. Although born in Mogadishu, I was reared in the United States. Our family fled to America to escape the violence that engulfed Somalia as it degenerated into civil war and state failure. I went to college in Minnesota, and graduate school at Johns Hopkins University in Washington, DC.

I include this personal history because in the aftermath of the cruel attack on civilians at the Westgate Shopping Mall in Nairobi, some reports suggest one or more Somali-Americans, perhaps from Minneapolis, may have participated in the attack. As once a member of the Somali diaspora in America, I want to assure subcommittee members, and indeed all Americans, that the overwhelming majority of Somalis living in the United States love and respect this country and are indebted to it for the opportunities it has provided to them. They have nothing but contempt for the al-Shabaab terrorists and what they have done to Somalia and stand with all civilized nations in denouncing their actions.

The Heritage Institute for Policy Studies was established in Mogadishu in January 2013. It is Somalia's first independent, nonprofit, nonpartisan think tank. It aims to inform and influence public policy and practice through empirically based research and analysis, direct engagement with senior policymakers and advocacy through the media, and to promote a culture of learning and research in the Somali region. Our most recent publications are briefing papers recommending how the international community can support the Federal Republic of Somalia through the "New Deal" development assistance and option for resolving the crisis between the central government of the Federal Republic and the people of Lower Jubba, Middle Jubba, and Gedo regions. More on the institute is on its Web site: www.heritageinstitute.org

One year after the formation of the first nontransitional government in over 20 years, there are reasons to be cautiously optimistic about the future of Somalia. The Somali people are determined, more than ever, to reclaim their dignity and, above all, their place among the community of nations.

They have also identified a common enemy to peace and stability. Citizens across the country are countering al-Shabaab's destruction and despair with construction and hope. Signs of economic vibrancy are re-emerging. The Somali diaspora are returning in large numbers, bringing with them much-needed skills, business opportunities and, most importantly, a sense of normalcy. Significant parts of Somalia, such as Somaliland in the northwest and Puntland in the northeast, are enjoying relative peace, stability and self-governance.

With regards to security, gains are less encouraging. Despite losing control of most major cities in Somalia, al-Shabaab fighters remain a major threat to peace and stability. The capital, Mogadishu, where I came from 2 days ago, is under constant assault. Grenade attacks, assassinations, suicide bombings, and JED attacks remain all too common. And as the recent Nairobi attack demonstrates, the Shabaab remains a lethal force as a militia in an asymmetrical warfare.

A key challenge to the restoration of stability is the chronic weakness of the security apparatuses. Command, control, and coordination is demonstrably weak due to the fragmentation of militias forming the security forces. Training, especially on protection of vulnerable civilians, remains poor and uncoordinated with various countries running programs. The composition of forces does not reflect the regional and clan diversity of the Somali people, depriving the security forces of a much-needed legitimacy. This is largely due to the unintended consequences of liberating parts of the country from al-Shabaab, and recruiting from these regions.

The U.S. Government has provided much-needed support to Somalia's struggling security forces, and the African Union's peacekeeping mission for many years. This support, from the U.S. and other development partners, is literally all that stands between the collapse of the Federal Government and its survival.

The U.S. Government must, however, utilize its support innovatively. Tactical counterterrorism measures, surgical strikes, and the provision of ammunition were necessary for sometime, but now there is a greater need for strategic partnership. Resources must now be channeled toward rebuilding competent, professional, accountable and broadly representative Somali security services with clear command and control. In order to defeat al-Shabaab, the Somali security forces need to be given a qualitative advantage over their enemy. At the moment, both sides are using mainly AK47s and RPGs. Armored personnel carriers, night vision goggles and air capability would be necessary.

AMISOM has done an excellent job of recovering regions from the Shabaab's tyranny, but they cannot become a substitute for indigenous forces. Somali forces can ultimately defeat al-Shabaab.

Security is inextricably linked to political accommodation and reconciliation, which is partially why Somalia adopted a federal model of governance nearly 10 years ago. But a consensus on which type of federalism remains elusive. Successive governments have failed to translate the federal vision into practical and viable member states. Frustrated with lack of progress at the national level, communities across the country have taken matters into their own hands, and carved out fiefdoms along clan lines. The American Dual Track Policy, which led to direct U.S. engagement with subnational entities, sent the wrong signal that the international community was promoting sectarian polities at the expense of a contiguous, federal government. Regional administrations practically run their affairs like independent states with virtually no input from the federal government.

The process of federating the country faces three enormous challenges. First, the Provisional Constitutional is deeply ambiguous and contradictory about the shape of the future Federal Government of Somalia, and division of powers between the center and peripheries. The meaning of federalism is broadly misunderstood by the Somali people, many of whom are legitimately worried about an overly centralized state, much like the military regime of Siyad Barre. This is compounded by the absence of an effective judicial branch that can interpret constitutional provisions.

The ambiguity of the Provisional Constitution has allowed political elites to interpret it to suit their own narrow interests. Consequently, existing and emerging member states are being formed with little or no consideration to economic, political, and social viability of the state, and with a deeply worrying lack of inclusivity and transparency. Rights of unarmed clans and minorities are routinely ignored, and processes to establish federal member states are done in the most secretive fashion.

Second, state institutions intended to play a leading role in national dialogue and the design of a suitable and agreeable federal structure are yet to be established. The Provisional Constitution calls for the formation of nearly a dozen independent commissions, half of which are instrumental to the federation process, such as the Boundaries and Federation Commission, the Inter-state Commission, and the Constitution Review and Implementation Commission. The Federal Government is far behind schedule on the establishment of these commissions.

These delays are inexcusable. The Federal Government garnered an unprecedented support from the Somali people following its inauguration in September 2012. It also won an unparalleled backing from the international community, including formal recognition by the U.S. Government for the first time in 20 years, easing of the U.N. arms embargo, monthly direct budgetary support from Turkey, and an expanded African Union Peacekeeping Mission.

Many Somalis believe that the Federal Government has fallen short of using that positive momentum to advance inclusive politics and dialogue with key domestic actors, including existing and emerging federal member states, traditional elders, and civil society.

Third, neighboring countries are undermining national reconciliation efforts by encouraging and sometimes helping with the formation of more subnational entities to suit their own domestic interests. Jubbaland was the most recent example. It was no secret that Kenya has organized, financed, and lobbied the international community to recognize the establishment of a "buffer zone" in its border with Somalia. While Ethiopia and Kenya face real threats from Somalia—as we've witnessed in the recent appalling attack in Nairobi—their unchecked interference risks further destabilizing of the country and a reversal of recent fragile gains.

The Provisional Constitution of Somalia envisions elections to take place toward the end of 2016. While this is not impossible, it's highly improbable given the magnitude of the tasks ahead. It should remain an admirable goal for the current government, but we must not substitute state-building for process-building. Elections are not an end in themselves, but rather a means toward the significantly more important objective of viable state formation, including finalizing the constitution, settling on a federal structure and adopting political party laws. In the absence of these steps, preparing for elections is a futile exercise.

The challenges facing the processes of federation and political consolidation in Somalia are tremendous, but not insurmountable.

First, the Provisional Constitution is a deeply flawed document that contradicts itself and puts future member states and the federal government on a direct collision course. The Somali people and their government need urgent assistance in this regard.

Priority must be given to the formation of the Review and Implementation Commission and Boundaries and Federation Commission. Once established, they will need considerable financial and human resources to engage in genuine national dialogue. There are a number of American institutions with relevant experience that can provide essential support in this area.

Second, assistance to the Somali Government must be contingent upon measurable gains. It must be held accountable to the Provisional Constitution and its own national plan. The culture of willfully missing constitutional deadlines must not be tolerated. If none of commissions is established by early next year, the Somali people will lose faith in the government's commitment to offer something more than its predecessors.

Somalis are rightfully worried that important transitional tasks will remain unfinished in 3 years when the government's mandate comes to an end. Without strong support from the U.S. and other development partners there is a grave risk of the country slipping back into chaos. The United States and its allies must seize this opportunity to consolidate recent gains.

The U.S. and its allies should assist the Somali people to develop mechanisms to hold their government to account. Somali civil society has always been, and will continue to be a powerful force for progress. The role of the civil society is currently worryingly absent. Civil society institutions must be strengthened and given the tools they need to effectively monitor the progress and integrity of the government. Properly amplified internal voices can induce change from within.

Third, as an important ally to both Ethiopia and Kenya, the United States has a moral obligation to exert pressure on the two countries to allow the Somali people and their government to engage in a national reconciliation. Interference galvanizes militant groups and further divides Somali communities.

The U.S. should certainly continue to assist both countries in mitigating the security threats they face. But Kenya and Ethiopia must realize that a democratic, strong, and vibrant Somali state on their borders is the greatest guarantor of security and prosperity in the region.

It is, at times, easy to dismiss Somalia as being irreparable, the archetypal failed state beyond hope. But as those of us who have given up their comfortable lives and families in the diaspora to return home can attest to, progress is possible. And it is happening across the country.

Somalia has made a profound leap from where it was just 3½ years ago, when I first started returning home. At the time, al-Shabaab controlled 75 percent of Mogadishu and almost 60 percent of the entire nation. Pirates were disrupting global shipping lanes. The very notion of government was contested across the country.

With the support of international partners like the United States, the European Union, the African Union, the United Kingdom, Turkey, and others, Somalia is slowly emerging from the abyss. What it needs now is relentless efforts to rebuild inclusive state institutions that have the legitimacy, capacity, and resources needed to finish the mammoth tasks ahead.

Senator COONS. Thank you very much, Mr. Aynte.
Dr. Hogendoorn.

STATEMENT OF DR. E.J. HOGENDOORN, DEPUTY DIRECTOR FOR AFRICA, INTERNATIONAL CRISIS GROUP, WASHINGTON, DC

Dr. HOGENDOORN. Thank you, Senator Coons and Senator Flake, for this opportunity.

Crisis Group has been working on Somalia since 2002 from our office in Nairobi, and we frequently travel to the country for research purposes.

Conditions in Somalia have improved. AMISOM, now including Kenya, has with the help of Ethiopia, the Somali National Army, the Sufi group, Ahlu Sunna wal Jamaa, and various allied clan militias, dealt al-Shabaab a serious strategic setback. Somalia also has a new albeit provisional government that is qualitatively better than previous administrations. The international community quickly recognized this government, and in September it pledged $2.5 billion in support.

However, the federal government only has de facto control over Mogadishu and parts of the south. Al-Shabaab is down but not out. It controls huge swaths of south and central Somalia and it still is able to hit high-profile targets.

The government also needs donors to pay security forces and to rebuild. Security in Mogadishu and elsewhere remains dependent on AMISOM and will likely for some time to come.

Neither AMISOM nor the government can impose a peace. Stability is only possible through a nationwide process of negotiation, power-sharing, and improved governance.

Arguably, Somalia's most intractable issue is the question of federalism. Simply put, there remains serious disagreement between those who would like to see Somalia become a strong unitary state, one that can stand up to its neighbors, and those that fear a centralized government would be dominated by a single clan or group of clans, as it was during the Siad Barre era.

Agreement on the powers of the federal government needs to be thrashed out quickly, otherwise Somalia risks embarking on a disruptive, piecemeal approach in the establishment of local administrations and federal states. The federal government quickly ran into trouble on the issue of federalism in Jubaland in southern Somalia, which was exacerbated by ambiguity in the constitution about who leads the process of creating these states.

Neighboring countries also have significant security interests in Somalia, and all have sizeable forces in the country. Beyond the Horn, Muslim Somalia is very much linked to the Middle East, and Egypt, Qatar, and Turkey are very active in the country.

Ethiopia is Somalia's historic rival. Addis Ababa, promoting its own system of ethnic federalism, is a strong proponent of federalism and a seemingly logical, bottom-up approach of state-building in Somalia. However, many Somalis see this as a ploy to keep their country weak and divided and are, thus, wary of international pressure to devolve power.

Kenya forcefully intervened in 2011 to create its own buffer state and facilitate the return of nearly half a million Somali refugees. It subsequently joined AMISOM but often follows its own interests. In Jubaland, Kenya has thrown its support behind Ahmed Madobe and not the federal government. Publicly Kenya is looking for an exit, but Somalis view this claim with great skepticism. According to the U.N. monitoring group, Kenyan politicians and officers are earning money from the trade, including banned charcoal passing through Kismayo. And more important, most believe Kenya wants to control southern Somalia because it has large oil and natural gas deposits.

Al-Shabaab is aggressively trying to turn the local population against what it calls Christian Kenyan occupiers, and the Westgate Mall attack was an attempt to trigger a crackdown to that end.

Beyond the regional states, a number of Muslim countries have taken an active interest in Somalia. This greater regional interest allows Somalia to play different states off against each other, particularly Muslim states against Ethiopia.

International cooperation is also complicated by a host of international organizations, including the United Nations, the African Union, and EGAD, the regional organization in East Africa, with no clear division of responsibilities or a lead actor.

The greatest problem was, and arguably remains, the overlapping mandate of the AU and the United Nations. The AU has the military peace enforcement responsibility, but by virtue of having been in Mogadishu for the last 4 years in fielding a force of over 17,000 troops, it is a political actor. While the U.N. has a political mandate, it is very much involved in security policy, security sector reform, and the vexing issue of federalism. Both missions are also headed by special representatives who reportedly get on well, but they and their staff have no clear instructions on how to share responsibilities.

The Westgate Mall attack. Much has been written about the latest terrorist attack. It is, however, important to note that this has long been expected and was certainly not the first, only the most destructive. It is important that the Kenyan Government prevent a backlash against its Somali and Muslim population, lest it does exactly what al-Shabaab was seeking.

What should the United States do in the opinion of Crisis Group?

First of all, it should support and prioritize nationwide negotiations on the type of federalism this federal government will implement and insist that the formation of new states adhere to a rule-based process. It should continue to support local and regional administrations' capacity-building, but this must be linked to reconciliation and measures to ensure minority clans are adequately represented in those governments.

Currently it is very difficult for aid agencies to provide development assistance in insecure areas. Yet, it is in these areas where assistance can be of the greatest benefit. Congress should consider supporting a smaller, high-risk but high-reward fund managed by the Office for Transition Initiatives for symbolic projects in Somalia's periphery.

Congress should also note that the 2016 elections are not far away. They are already behind schedule, and election assistance should be quickly funded by donors.

More attention should also be given to countering radicalization in Somalia and the horn. The United States should be giving quiet assistance to such programs.

The U.S. Government should also place much greater emphasis on reconciliation, both with armed factions and on a national level between clans. It should provide support for local peace and reconciliation conferences that can feed into larger regional conferences.

It should also provide the new U.N. mission, UNSOM, with all the capacity necessary to coordinate assistance effectively, and it should insist that the federal government does so effectively as well.

The State Department and DOD should also start working with AMISOM to clearly articulate a multiyear exit strategy for its intervention in Somalia, and this should be linked with incremental support to the creation of a professional, mixed-clan national army.

Last, the United States should convene an international working group to help create a transparent mechanism to monitor revenue collection in Somalia's major ports and airports, including an oversight board with a mixed international and Somali composition and supported by experts, as was done in Liberia, to ensure that port revenue is used to develop all regions in Somalia equitably.

In conclusion, Somalia remains an extremely weak and fragile state. Its security is dependent on external sources. Its sovereignty is threatened, and its stability is far from certain. Yet, it is at an inflection point where the hope of achieving sustainable progress is becoming real if, and only if, the international community works together toward that goal and Somalis honestly confront the governance challenges facing their country.

I thank you and look forward to your questions.

[The prepared statement of Dr. Hogendoorn follows:]

PREPARED STATEMENT OF DR. E.J. HOGENDOORN

I would like to take this opportunity to thank the Chairman Coons and the other members of the Senate Foreign Relations Subcommittee on African Affairs for inviting Crisis Group to testify today on Security and Governance in Somalia. Crisis Group has been working on Somalia since 2002, and has produced some 18 in-depth reports and briefings on the conflict there and continues to follow events there closely from our office in Nairobi, with frequent visits to the country's various regions.

Crisis Group is an independent, nonpartisan, nongovernmental organization that provides field-based analysis, policy advice, and recommendations to governments, the United Nations, the European Union, and other multilateral organizations on the prevention and resolution of deadly conflict. Crisis Group was founded in 1995 by distinguished diplomats, statesmen, and opinion leaders including Career Ambassador, Mort Abramowitz; Nobel Prize winner and former Finnish President, Martti Ahtisaari; late Congressman, Stephen Solarz; and former U.N. and British diplomat, Mark Malloch-Brown.

Ambassador Thomas Pickering is our current chairman. Louise Arbour, former chief prosecutor at the International Criminal Tribunals for Rwanda and for the former Yugoslavia, and past U.N. High Commissioner for Human Rights, is our current president. In 2011, Crisis Group was awarded the Eisenhower Medal for Leadership and Service.

Crisis Group publishes some 80 reports and briefing papers annually, as well as a monthly CrisisWatch bulletin. Our staff is located on the ground in 10 regional offices, and 16 other locations, covering between them over 60 countries and focused on conflict prevention and post-conflict peace-building. We maintain advocacy and research offices in Brussels (our global headquarters), Washington, and New York. We have liaison offices in London, Beijing, and Moscow.

THE SITUATION IN SOMALIA

Conditions have improved in the last several years. The African Union Mission for Somalis (AMISOM), now including Kenya, has with the help of Ethiopia, the Somali National Army (SNA), the Sufi Ahlu Sunna wal Jamaa, and various clan militia allies dealt the armed Islamist fundamentalist group Harakat al-Shabaab al-Mujahedeen (Mujahidin Youth Movement), better known as al-Shabaab a serious strategic setback by formally ejecting it from Mogadishu, Afgooye, Baidoa, Merca, and Kismayo (it still has an underground presence in these cities). This represents a huge psychological blow and has deprived the group of major revenue sources. Al-Shabaab has also been weakened by internal conflict, and several large and important factions have left the organization. Mogadishu, although it continues to be plagued by assassinations and occasionally larger asymmetrical attacks, is more secure; resulting in thousands of residents returning, and a torrent of business investment in the city's reconstruction.

Somalia also has a new, albeit still interim government that is qualitatively better than previous administrations. Neither President Hassan Sheikh nor Prime Minister Abdi Shirdoon played major roles in civil war. They appointed a relatively lean and technocratic Cabinet. In addition, the new 225-member Parliament is more representative than previous iterations.

The Somali Federal Government (SFG) also developed a ''Six Pillar'' strategy that focuses on stability, economic recovery, peace-building, international relations, and national unity. Optimism led the international community, including the U.S., to quickly recognize the new government and in September it pledged some $2.5 billion in ''New Deal'' support that, conditioned on greater transparency and governance reforms, will go through the SFG. If allocated efficiently, this money could be a huge boon to the country and its people.

A REALITY CHECK

Despite all its good will, the SFG is still a provisional government, with de facto control only over Mogadishu and parts of the South, and dependent on foreign troops to keep its enemies at bay. Al-Shabaab is down but not out. It controls, or at least is able to operate at will in, huge swaths of south and central Somalia, and still able to hit high-profile targets in Mogadishu's heavily fortified areas, including the national courts, the U.N. compound, the Turkish Embassy, and popular gathering places such as the Village restaurant. Somalia also remains an extremely poor country, the SFG generates very few of its own resources, and is largely dependent on the international community to pay its security forces and begin the difficult and very expensive task of rebuilding after nearly 20 years of state collapse. A lot of the taxes and fees on trade transiting through ports and airports (the major sources of official revenue) is still "captured" by corrupt officials and local clans and businessmen. Furthermore, the international community has pumped hundreds of millions of dollars into security sector reform since 2000, with little tangible positive impact and arguably exacerbated instability. Security in Mogadishu, and elsewhere, remains dependent on AMISOM, and will likely for some time to come.

Yet AMISOM alone, with some 17,000 troops cannot pacify an area the size of New Mexico. The government also cannot stabilize Somalia through military measures alone—it cannot impose a peace—it must recognize its limitations and accept that stability is only possible through a nationwide process of negotiation, power-sharing with other political forces and improved governance.

Al-Shabaab also remains a potent threat, as demonstrated by Westgate Mall operation in Nairobi, and high profile attacks in Mogadishu and elsewhere. Ahmed Godane appears to have taken firm control of the organization and seems intent on regionalizing his operations. Al-Shabaab is a serious regional threat and has links to other extremist groups in the Horn and the continent. "Hard" counterterrorist measures can only be so good, it will be extremely difficult for regional states, the SFG, and AMISOM to protect soft targets from terrorist attacks.

THE CHALLENGE OF FEDERALISM

Arguably the most intractable issue is the question of federalism. Despite 5 years of work, the committee drafting Somalia's new constitution was unable to reconcile different positions on the devolution of power and left many provisions on federalism vague or unaddressed in the provisional constitution that forms the basic law of the SFG. Put simplistically, serious disagreements remain between those who would like to see Somalia become a strong unitary state—one that can stand up to neighbors, such as Ethiopia, that have long meddled in its affairs—and those that fear a centralized government would be dominated by a single clan, or group of clans—as it was during the Siad Barre era—and would then deny them their fair share of resources. This divide also tends to follow clan lines with many Hawiye clans, who dominate central and south Somalia and particularly greater Mogadishu, supporting a unitary state, while many Darod clans, who dominate Puntland and Jubaland, are strong proponents of federalism.

Agreement on the powers of the federal government need to be thrashed out quickly, otherwise Somalia risks embarking on a "piece-meal" approach in the establishment of local administrations and federal states. The SFG quickly ran into trouble on the issue of federalism, exacerbated by ambiguity in the constitution about who leads the process of creating states. Instead of building its own legitimacy by focusing on the service provision in Mogadishu and other liberated areas, or working with de-facto authorities, the SFG forcefully inserted itself into the Jubaland process, in far away Kismayo, southern Somalia, by appointing its own district-level officials (as was allowed by the constitution). The local authorities ignored the SFG (and the constitution), convened a conference, and ultimately elected a former al-Shabaab commander, but now Ethiopian and Kenyan ally, Ahmed Mohamed Islam "Madobe" in April. Pushed by proponents of a strong central state, the SFG continued ratcheting up the pressure and at one point al-Shabaab militias allowed pro-SFG forces to move troops and "technicals" through their territory on the way to Kismayo. Barre Hiraale, a SFG ally (and a former proxy of Ethiopia) even publicly announced that his forces were colocated with al-Shabaab and planning joint operations against Madobe. Several violent clashes followed, and only under concerted pressure from Ethiopia, Kenya, and the international community were the two sides able to reach a tentative agreement, in Addis Ababa, on the establishment of the Jubaland Interim Administration: with Madobe the President for no more than 2 years and a promise that the SFG would take control of Kismayo port and airport, provided the revenues would remain in the region. The agreement was guaranteed by Ethiopia as chair of the Intergovernment Authority on Development (IGAD), the regional security organization. Somalia's neighbors thus facilitated the peace, but at the same time also are laying the ground for further conflict.

This week Madobe, beholden to his Ogaden clan, refused to meet the SFG per the Addis Ababa Agreement's terms, and thus seemingly rejected it. Jubaland is very much an Ogaden-dominated state, and if the interim administration is not careful it will drive alienate minority clans from the region to support al-Shabaab or other armed opposition groups. Kenya in particular may then be pulled into supporting an increasingly unpopular regional government, which could be further exploited by al-Shabaab to characterize its intervention as an "occupation" (much like it did the Ethiopian intervention from 2006–2009) and Madobe as a puppet. It must be the

SFG's role to represent the interests of minority clans, and not allow dominant clans to dictate particular state's political dispensations.

The region has significant security interests in Somalia, and immediate neighbors Djibouti, Ethiopia, Kenya, and Uganda all have sizable forces in the country. Beyond the Horn, Muslim Somali is very much linked into the Middle East, and Egypt, Qatar, and Turkey are very active in the country.

Despite its size, Djibouti plays a significant role, in large part because much of its population is Somali and many Somali businessmen either do business in, or have strong ties with businessmen from the country. Djibouti has also hosted several multiyear Somali peace processes and its elite have strong ties to Somali leaders. Its forces are now based in relatively quiet central Somalia.

Ethiopia has been Somalia's historic regional rival: disputes over control of the Ogaden region, which Somali nationalists consider to be part of "Greater Somalia" continue, and led to a brief war (1977–78) and much longer proxy conflict. Calls for the annexation of the Ogaden, as well as other parts of greater Somalia, remain popular with Somali nationalists, and pandering to this sentiment by the Islamic Court Union (ICU) was part of the reason Ethiopia intervened in Somalia in 2006. Addis Ababa quickly expelled the ICU from major cities, and then remained to prop up the then Transitional Federal Government (TFG). This led to the rise of al-Shabaab, which presented itself as the most effective force fighting Ethiopian "occupation." It was during this period that the group received its most significant diaspora support—not because they shared its ideology, but because they saw al-Shabaab as part of a liberation struggle. The intervention cost Ethiopia dearly, and 3 years later, Addis quietly relented to the selection of Sheikh Sharif Sheikh Ahmed, the former chairman of the ICU as the new TFG President. Ethiopia quickly withdrew, with AMISOM only slowly replacing it as the force protecting the embattled government. Since then Ethiopia has focused largely on supporting groups that can effectively act as a buffer along its borders, many of whom are resistant to the new central government. This includes Somaliland and Puntland State.

Ethiopia, promoting its own system of "ethnic federalism" is a strong proponent of federalism in Somalia, and has long supported a seemingly logical "bottom up" approach of state-building. Many Somalis, however, see this as a ploy to keep their country weak and divided, and this very much plays into the hostility of many toward international pressure for the SFG to truly devolve power. While overstated, Ethiopia is wary of a strong Somali central state, particularly if it is close to countries perceived as hostile by Addis Ababa.

Kenya is a relatively new entrant in Somalia. Nairobi forcefully intervened in 2011 to create its own buffer state and facilitate the return of more than 0.5 million Somali refugees currently living in the country. Kenya subsequently joined AMISOM, but often follows its own interests. In Jubaland, Kenya has thrown its support behind Ahmed Madobe, its most effective proxy force leader. Publicly Kenya is looking for an exit, but Somalis view this claim with great scepticism. According to the U.N. Monitoring Group, Kenyan-Somali politicians and Kenyan military officers are allegedly earning large amounts of money from trade, including illegal charcoal, passing through Kismayo, and more importantly most believe Kenya wants to control southern Somalia because it has large oil and natural gas deposits. Al-Shabaab is aggressively trying to turn the local population against the Kenyan "Christian" forces occupiers, and the Westgate Mall attack was an attempt to trigger a crackdown to that end.

Uganda is most removed, but remains the dominant actor in Mogadishu (despite the presence of a large Burundian continent) because of the size of its contingent and the forceful personality of President Museveni. It contingent is also accused by Somalis of profiteering from the war. Previously very active, Museveni lately has been distracted by political turmoil in Kampala and has taken a less force role, ceding some influence to Ethiopia and Kenya.

Beyond the regional states, a number of Muslim countries have taken an active interest in Somalia. Turkey is perhaps the most prominent country, and to its credit played a major role in responding to the latest famine in 2011, and then subsequently has arrogated a substantial role for itself, and its companies, in the reconstruction efforts. Qatar has also played a major role, particularly in its support for President Hassan Sheikh Mohamud and his supporters from Damul Jadiid (New Blood), a faction of Al-Islaah, the Somali wing of the Muslim Brotherhood. The emergence of the Muslim Brotherhood has also increased the interest of Egypt, which before Tharir Square had been in major competition with Ethiopia over influence in Somalia. The greater regional interest allows the SFG to play different states off each other, particularly Muslim states against Ethiopia. The influence of Damul Jadiid has led Somalia to re-orient somewhat away from IGAD and AU toward Middle East. This has complicated Somalia's relationship with Ethiopia and Kenya, and to a degree with the U.N.

Not only is international involvement complicated by numerous bilateral countries with individual agendas, but there are also a number of international organizations, including the U.N., AU, and IGAD (not to forget, occasionally, the League of Arab States, the World Bank, and NATO) active in Somalia with no clear division of responsibilities or lead actor. (This sometimes was a problem within the U.N. and AMISOM as well, where agencies did not cooperate or contingents did not follow the chain of command). They are also joined by a number of special envoys with unclear roles vis a vis the international organizations, the missions in Somalia or ambassadors accredited to Mogadishu.

The greatest problem was, and arguably remains, the overlapping mandates of the AU and the U.N. The AU has the military peace enforcement responsibility, but by virtue of having been in Mogadishu for the last 4 years and fielding a force of over 17,000 troops is a major political actor in Somalia, while the U.N. has a political mandate, but by virtue of security being a huge part of reestablishing stability in the country (as well as supply a great deal of support to AMISOM, through UNSOA, and the government) was very much involved in security policy and security sector reform. Both missions are also headed by special representatives with no clear instructions on how to share responsibilities. This was a particular problem for AMISOM and UNPOS, particularly because UNPOS was based in Kenya and its senior staff rarely spent much time in Mogadishu.

It is too early to tell if new United Nations Assistance Mission for Somalia (UNSOM), established on 3 June 2012 can succeed where so many others have failed. Its mandate includes the provision of policy advice to the SFG and AMISOM on peace-building and state-building in the areas of: governance, security sector reform and rule of law (including the disengagement of combatants), development of a federal system (including preparations for elections in 2016), and coordination of international donor support. It is also tasked to help build the SFG's capacity to promote respect for human rights and women's empowerment, promote child protection, prevent conflict-related sexual and gender-based violence, and strengthen justice institutions. To strengthen intra-U.N. coordination, a major problem since UNPOS was created in 1995, a post of the Deputy Special Representative of the Secretary-General/Resident and Humanitarian Coordinator will be established on 1 January 2014 and ''structurally integrated into UNSOM.''

Importantly, UNSOM is based in Mogadishu and will be deployed across Somalia, as requested by the Federal Government and as conditions permitted—so far it is only present in the capital, Garowe, Baidoa and Kismayo (it has not received permission to establish an office in Hargeisa). The Security Council emphasized the need for coordination, and UNSOM and AMISOM will work ''on parameters for practical partnership on the ground.'' To date UNSOM is just starting to deploy with approximately 50 staff in Mogadishu, whose mobility is severely subscribed because of insecurity (the U.N. compound was attacked on 19 June and 1 permanent staff, 3 contractors and 4 guards were killed, along with at least 6 Somali bystanders). It will not be up to full strength until early 2014, depending on the security situation.

The major role for UNSOM will be coordinating security sector reform and international support. As was noted by the U.N. technical assessment team, ''A common and closely coordinated strategy for international security support, which sets out clearly the respective responsibilities for the Africa Union, the United Nations, other allies, and Somali forces, with clear timelines and appropriate resources is a priority.'' Security training is now being conducted by Somali forces, the European Union Training Mission (EUTM), Turkey, Ethiopia, and Bancroft Global Development, a private company. This is ostensibly coordinated through a UNSOM facilitated and Somali-led steering group. Much work remains to be done. According to the last U.N. report, Somali forces continue to face significant logistical challenges and ''indiscipline continued to present a challenge, and there were reports of clashes within Somali security forces in Baidoa and Buurhakaba, and an increasing number of desertions in Bay and Bakool. Furthermore, police continue to face serious capacity gaps and ''international support, including stipends and training continues, but lack of coherence undermines its effectiveness.''

Donor coordination will be equally challenging. Encouragingly the SFG has developed the Somali Compact that strives to provide an overarching strategic framework for coordinating political, security and development efforts over the next 3 years. It will remain to be seen if the donor community, in its New Deal pledges, will adhere to that framework, especially as counterterrorism priorities again rise to the fore with the recent Westgate Mall attack.

THE WESTGATE ATTACK

Much has already been written about the latest al-Shabaab attack in Nairobi. It is however important to note that it had long been expected, and it was certainly not the first, only the most destructive, with consequently the most media attention. Since Kenyan troops went into Somalia, militia groups have launched some 50 attacks into northeastern Kenya, and a number of grenade attacks in Mombasa and Nairobi. Almost all seem to have been aimed at creating a backlash against Kenyan Somalis and Muslims, deepening sectarian divisions and driving those populations to provide more support to radical Islamist groups. A related goal was to put pressure on Kenya to withdraw its forces from southern Somalia, either because it was unwilling to pay the price at home, or because the local population was turning against AMISOM. It is therefore important that the Kenyan Government prevent a backlash against its Somali and Muslim population, lest it does exactly what al-Shabaab was seeking.

WHAT THE U.S. CAN DO

- Support and prioritize nationwide negotiations on the type federalism the SFG will implement. Insist that the formation of new states adheres to a rule-based process.
- Continue to support local and regional administrations' capacity-building, particularly through the Local Stability Fund proposed by the U.K. at the London Conference in 2012, but this must be linked to reconciliation and measures to ensure minority clans are adequately represented in those governments.
- It is very difficult for aid agencies to provide development assistance in insecure areas of Somalia, yet it is in these areas where assistance can have the greatest marginal benefit, particularly for nascent local administrations. Congress should consider supporting a ''venture development fund'' managed by OTI to provide small and quick high risk, but high reward grants for symbolic projects, such as medical clinics and boreholes, focused on local governments in Somalia's periphery. Such projects would provide much-needed services and much-needed legitimacy to local authorities and a tangible reward for withdrawing support from al-Shabaab. This is what many Islamic NGOs are doing in Somalia.
- The 2016 elections are not so far away. Crucial constitutional commissions, such as Boundaries Commission and Independent Constitutional Review Commission, are not yet established. If there are many setbacks, it is quite likely the polls will have to be delayed, which will be extremely destabilizing. (The SFG's vision 2016, is already signaling the need for contingency plans if one-person-one-vote elections are not possible at that time.) Election assistance should already be funded by donors. Thought should also be given to piloting smaller municipal elections.
- More attention should be given to countering radicalization in Somalia and the Horn. The U.S. should give quiet assistance to programs that articulate the argument that radicalisation is largely driven by a unique set of beliefs alien to Somalis and an extremist and literal interpretation of holy texts.
- Help develop effective, long-term counter- and de-radicalisation strategies for all the countries in the Horn of Africa. As Crisis Group noted in ''Kenyan Somali Islamist Radicalisation'' (25 January 2012), a link exists between radicalization and terrorism, but counterterrorism tactics aimed only at stopping al-Shabaab and other militant groups should not become the only official response. Counter-radicalization—reducing the appeal of radicalism—and de-radicalization—persuading people who are already in radical organisations to leave them—are long-term processes that require tact and patience.
- Place much greater emphasis on reconciliation, both with armed factions and on a national level between clans. Provide support to local peace and reconciliation conferences that can feed into larger regional conferences only after most local disputes have been resolved. These conferences should be completed before elections.
- Provide UNSOM with all the capacity necessary to coordination assistance effectively. Insist that the SFG does so effectively as well.
- Have the State Department and DOD work with AMISOM to clearly articulate a multiyear exit strategy for its intervention in Somalia. This should be linked

with incremental support to the creation of a professional, mixed-clan national army.

- Develop a mechanism with AMISOM to coordinate the activities of allied local administration security forces. This should run in parallel to negotiations on the roles and responsibilities of the regional, state, and federal governments.
- Because no one knows how much revenue is generate by individual ports and airports, much conflict in Somalia is over assumed revenue flows and the division thereof. As Crisis Group suggested in "The Kenyan Military Intervention in Somalia" (15 February 2012), the international community should convene an international working group to help create a mechanism to transparently monitor revenue collection Somalia's major ports and airports, particularly in Bossaso, Mogadishu, Merca, and Kismayo, including an oversight board with mixed international and Somali composition and supported by experts (forensic accountants) and international customs officers, much as was done in Liberia; and ensure that the revenue is used to develop all regions in Somalia.

CONCLUSION

The SFG remains an extremely weak and fragile state, its security dependent on external sources, its sovereignty threatened and its stability far from certain. Yet it is at an inflection point where the hope of achieving sustainable progress is becoming real if, and only if, the international community work together to that goal and Somalis honestly confront the governance challenges facing their country.

Senator COONS. Thank you, Dr. Hogendoorn.

Let me start with your last of many recommendations first and work back to the previous.

First, I will ask of all three of you a question about sort of the security situation and the financing of al-Shabaab and what are the strategic challenges we face and then, second, about federalism. All three of you had some interesting comments about federalism.

On the first question, my sense is that al-Shabaab has been principally financed through the charcoal trade when they controlled Kismayo and parts of the coastline and through the extraction of taxes from those communities they control. And the U.N. monitoring group I think recently described how the regional charcoal trade helps finance al-Shabaab.

What should we be doing here forward to ensure that al-Shabaab loses the financial support to continue operations, and what do you see as the most important next steps to strengthen AMISOM to actually carry out its mission of stabilizing the security of the country to make possible a transition to a more broadly, representative, inclusive and professionalized Somali national forces? I would be interested in all three of your answers to that set of questions. Dr. Hogendoorn, Mr. Aynte, Dr. Le Sage, in order please.

Dr. HOGENDOORN. As I mentioned before, the charcoal trade is actually banned by the U.N. Security Council, and I think that the United States should do more to force its partners to, in fact, adhere to those prohibitions.

I think that the real challenge with AMISOM is that it has essentially reached a point where it can no longer push farther out, and either the international community needs to provide more resources to AMISOM to increase its troop capacity and improve its ability to reach out or more needs to be done on the political side to try to stabilize Somalia.

Senator COONS. Mr. Aynte, thoughts on how we reduce financing to al-Shabaab by whatever means.

Mr. AYNTE. I think the first thing is we need to know exactly where the financing of al-Shabaab is coming from. And the conventional belief was that it was mostly coming from the cities that it controlled and the resources it controlled like the Bakaara market in Mogadishu and the port. Now that has gone, I think many of us are wondering where the financing still seems to be coming through. Part of the answer lies with the fact that they still control a considerable amount of land in south-central Somalia. So the immediate answer to that is an attempt to try to recapture that part of the land.

I do, though, in relation to this, want to emphasize the importance of really creating an indigenous security force. I think that is ultimately where the answer lies. It is considerably cheaper than the African Union peacekeeping mission, which is necessary and needed and has done a remarkable job up until this moment. But I think a serious attempt need to be made both by the Somali Government but by the international partners to try and rebuild a professional, inclusive, and competent security sector.

Senator COONS. What timeline do you think it is possible to rebuild a representative, credible, vetted Somali national security force?

Mr. AYNTE. It is certainly going to take a considerable amount of time in my view, and I think both the cases of Iraq and Afghanistan are quite instructive to Somalia both in terms of the timeframe that it could take, but also in the kinds of numbers that we need. You have hundreds of thousands of forces created and formed for Iraq and close to 300,000 for Afghanistan. Somalia has so far only 18,000 security services, half of which are probably engaged in VIP protection of individuals and installations. So clearly half of them are incapacitated from their main task of dealing with al-Shabaab.

Senator COONS. Dr. Le Sage, if you might, for AMISOM to be successful, they need—several of you have recommended greater force projection capability, both more advanced weapons systems and airlift and attack capabilities. If you might comment more both on what AMISOM needs to be successful, what we need to do to further restrict al-Shabaab's resources, and then what does the transition look like to a credible national Somali security force?

Dr. LE SAGE. Thank you, Senator.

Starting with the issue of al-Shabaab's funding, charcoal, when the movement controlled the port city of Kismayo, was the single largest foreign currency earner for the group, but it also generated revenues by controlling road junctions and levying taxes there, taxing at markets, and extorting money from businesses which otherwise could not operate.

Now al-Shabaab has lost control of Kismayo, but it remains very close by. So it can tax the charcoal trade at the source of production, rather than at the source of onward distribution. And in this sense, their control of the town of Barawe in Lower Shabelle really is critical. This affords them the opportunity to impact any trade that is coming from Mogadishu to Kismayo and tax it and also to still make revenue off of the charcoal business. So in that sense, more aggressive operations to actually dislodge al-Shabaab from Barawe and other key towns are really going to be the best and fastest way of degrading their revenue-earning ability and sustaining the movement in that sense.

It is absolutely true that AMISOM needs force multipliers, needs helicopters, needs additional transport, and potentially additional soldiers in order to undertake those movements. Right now, AMISOM forces are limited to the same number that they had when they only controlled the city of Mogadishu but they are spread out in multiple locations, Afgooye, Jowhar, Baidoa, many other cities. So they are stuck using that limited number of forces in a static security role.

The fastest way for them to actually free up those forces and be able to deploy them in an offensive operation would be if the Somali Federal Government worked with local administrations to actually craft consensual governance in the area. Local forces, particularly the Somali National Army or other militia forces, provide local security, and then let AMISOM take the fight toward al-Shabaab and other spoilers of the peace process.

Senator COONS. One question of all three of you on federalism. There seems to be a real tension between a desire for a strong national government to be able to resist intrusion from Ethiopia, from Kenya sort of meddling by outside forces, one perception goes. On the other hand, there is a suspicion of a strong federal or national government because of experiences under the Siad Barre government, because of the strength of clans, and because of the very different cultural and political traditions across the country.

Managing these with a constitution that in its current form has significant internal contradictions around what the federal structure should look like is quite difficult. It is very different from our own Articles of Confederation period, but there are some striking similarities in that moving toward a healthy and functioning national government for purposes of security, taxation, control of ports, control of trade is necessary, but there are significant internal concerns that mitigate against a strong unitary federal government.

What role should the U.S. Government be playing in advancing a federal structure, and did our dual track policy actually hurt that process? And what do you recommend for U.S. policy with regards to federalism and implementation going forward, if you could in order, Dr. Le Sage, Mr. Aynte, and Dr. Hogendoorn?

Dr. LE SAGE. Thank you, Senator.

The fact is that the Somali Federal Government right now is a key actor. It is the key actor going forward in making decisions for the establishment of a true federal system that actually provides some degree of convergence between the local actors in major towns across Somalia's regions and the central government. But the Somali Federal Government is currently only one actor on the scene. If we are talking about the locations where Kenya, Ethiopia, other AMISOM forces are operating, if we are talking about those places where we need to fight al-Shabaab, there are other actors of concern. This is the Jubaland authority, the interim Juba authority that has been established in Kismayo. This is Rahanweyn clan forces that are based in Baidoa working very closely with Ethiopia. It is the autonomous regional administration of Puntland and also the self-declared independent state of Somaliland. In addition, there are many other local administrations loyal to the Ahlu Sunna wal Jamaa movements or other smaller, sub-clan-based administrations. These are actually facts on the ground.

There has been a great deal of concern that the United States dual track approach was going to reinforce these and in some way dismember Somalia and it was going to make it a weaker country. The fact is 20-odd years of civil war have decentralized Somalia radically and made it a remarkably weak country. The dual track approach allowed the United States to engage both at the capital level and at that local administration regional level at the same time to promote an agenda of convergence.

Maybe the language needs to be changed at this point in time, but that ability to support both levels simultaneously is what is ultimately required to promote these power-sharing and resource-sharing deals internally within a town like Baidoa, but then between that town and the central government.

Senator COONS. Thank you.

Mr. AYNTE. Senator, that is a good question.

I think it is important to highlight that Somali people, wherever they are in Somalia today, do want some sort of a federal structure. It is just unclear in their mind. We are actually engaged in a research at the moment looking at this, and what we found are that there are universal demands for basic things in the debate on federalism. Every Somali wants to elect his or her local and national leaders. Secondly, they want to get government services closer to where they are. Thirdly, they want to see an equitable sharing of natural resources, and fourthly, they would like to see constitutional guarantees against government intrusion upon their individual and group rights.

We believe these are the four issues that can help and push forward the debate and the framework for federalism in Somalia.

What could the U.S. Government do?

I think the first thing is really the building and formations of the commissions that I talked about, the Independent Commission to Review the Constitution, the Boundaries and Federation Commission, and ultimately the Inter-State Commission. I think what these three commissions can then do with expertise from the United States and institutions that are capable is to lead a national dialogue. At the moment, there is virtually no dialogue about federalism at the national level. You know, politicians are talking to each other and mostly to advance a group or individual interests.

But I think what needs to happen is a national understanding of the options of federalism. When we interviewed people across the country about if they understood options on federalism and confederation and decentralized unitary state and devolution of power and all of these options, most people did not really understand what these options are. So I think a civic education process is really needed. But that needs to happen alongside the commissions.

The third step that the United States could help with is the finalization of the provisional constitution, which again is deeply ambiguous, contradictory in many ways.

So I think these three steps could be a strong starting point. Of course, it is unrealistic to expect that we will have a clearer picture

3 years from now, but I think we could be at a strong position 3 years from now.

Senator COONS. Thank you, Mr. Aynte.

Dr. Hogendoorn.

Dr. HOGENDOORN. Well, as we know, here in the United States, federalism remains an extremely contentious issue—even in these hallowed halls.

I would agree with Andre Le Sage and Abdi Aynte that perhaps we need to recast the dual track approach as perhaps the parallel approach.

But I think the important point is that the money cannot go to Mogadishu alone. If it goes to Mogadishu, it stays in Mogadishu as it is currently mostly. All the progress that we are seeing in Somalia is largely in Mogadishu and it is because all the resources that are being pledged to the country are largely staying in the capital. That is to some degree understandable. I think when the federal government is trying to do things, it is easier to do stuff in the capital than it would be to do in places far away, especially when they do not have formal links with these kinds of local administrations or they are in very hostile relationships with them as they have been with Jubaland.

I think the important point that people need to recognize is that al-Shabaab benefits from these disagreements and it benefits from these tensions. And one of the biggest problems is that while Jubaland is somewhat more stable and it is arguably less of a safe haven for al-Shabaab, the fact that Jubaland is being dominated by a single clan allows al-Shabaab to recruit from minority clans who feel that they are not being adequately represented by those local administrations. And to some degree, al-Shabaab is waiting that game in other areas as well, waiting to see those political tensions come to the fore and using that as an effective recruiting tool to rebuild its ranks.

Thank you.

Senator COONS. Thank you. Thank you for your answers to that question.

Senator Flake, thank you for your patience.

Senator FLAKE. Thank you. No problem. Those were a lot of the questions I had particularly on federalism.

Mr. Aynte, you kind of addressed it just now in your remarks. The provisional constitution is a deeply flawed document and contradicts itself. You were referring mostly to the federalism aspects of that?

Mr. AYNTE. Senator, it is all across, but the federalism is the most important element where it really contradicts and puts future federal member states on a collision course with the federal government in that it gives—the division of power between the periphery and the center is not clear in the document as it stands at the moment. But it is only provisional and it can be improved.

Senator FLAKE. You mentioned four things that you think are expected of people, what they expect out of a central government. Do those apply to the folks in Somaliland and Puntland as well? It sounds to me as if, speaking with some of their representatives, they do not want to share in the country's resources. They have their own. They want nothing to do with the rest of the country. Am I off base there or is that their assessment?

Mr. AYNTE. Senator, I think Somaliland and Puntland are slightly different.

I think Somaliland is seeking an outright secession from Somalia for the last 20 years. It has done a remarkable job of stabilizing itself, having a self-rule, and really laying the foundation for democratic institutions and democratic processes, of course, with some flaws.

Puntland is not seeking secession from the rest of the country, but it does—like other regions in Somalia, although in theory, it is under the federal government, in practice it is very much like Somaliland, carrying out its business entirely independently from the federal government. Again, this is because of the vacuum that exists with the federal government.

I do, though, think that if a concerted effort is made to clarify the constitution and begin this national dialogue on federalism, I think there is a real opportunity for engagement with Puntland and with other emerging and existing federal member states.

Senator FLAKE. The last panel was talking about the government there and at one point referred to it as a democratically elected government. It is not quite that simple. How is it viewed in the rest of the country?

I know going back to—what was it—1998 or so with the first attempt to appoint traditional elders who would appoint a constituent assembly of some type or the last kind of iteration of this experience, and it did not take hold. What makes this different here? Why is this government going to be viewed as anything different than the last attempt, Mr. Hogendoorn? Or is it?

Dr. HOGENDOORN. Well, I mean, I would agree with everyone or most observers that there were very significant flaws with this election process. That said, I think that there was a greater attempt to ensure that at least the majority of the elders who were at this constituent assembly—who then picked the Parliament; who then selected the President—were at least somewhat more representative than they had been in the past. It certainly was not a perfect process. There were lots of allegations of vote buying, of vote rigging, of extortion, and so on and so forth.

I think people focus mostly on the fact that the Prime Minister and the President who were selected—or at least the President who was elected and then the Prime Minister who was selected were both notably not involved in the civil war in any major way. And so this was kind of seen as a bit of a break from the past. And to be perfectly honest, the President especially was someone who came from civil society who we had worked with in the past, who many of us had worked with in the past and were quite excited about that possibility. That certainly does not mean that the government is perfect, but we certainly see it as an improvement on past regimes.

Senator FLAKE. How realistic is the 2016 timeframe for elections? We seem to have backed a horse now with this government. If it does not take place, what is our position? What do we do? Mr. Aynte, do you have thoughts there?

Mr. AYNTE. Well, as I said, I think elections are not impossible but highly improbable to take place in 2016, as we understand elections. We might be looking at another ''selectocracy'' as the 2012 was called by some people. It could be that we might have elections in parts that are a little more stable than others. But considering the slow pace of progress in the last year and the work that needs to be done, I would be pleasantly surprised if elections take place in 2016.

What are the options after that? Well, I think it will depend on what the stakeholders in Somalia want to do, the way forward. Of course, not many people are looking forward to the idea of extension. The ''E'' word is now seen as—you know, no one wants to hear that. But I think there has to be some sort of a selection process that then brings the country to the next level.

I should finally say, though, that the reason why this government is possibly seen as a little bit more hopeful than the previous ones is people are seeing this as one step toward the greater goal of consolidating the gains that have been made over the years, so part of an incremental process.

Senator FLAKE. Mr. Le Sage, with regard to the failed raid last week, the last panel did want to go there. What are the implications for the future? Does this embolden the elements we do not want to embolden? What happens? What are the practical effects of this? And did it surprise you that, one, we launched the raid and, two, it ended as it did?

Dr. LE SAGE. I think the most important recent development in terms of strengthening al-Shabaab and exacerbating the threat that the movement poses to the region is the Westgate attack. And we should not let the sensationalism, frankly, of the events over the weekend overshadow that tragedy and the precedent that that attack set for jihadists both within the East Africa region but potentially on a global scale not to undertake a suicide bombing operation that is highly complicated, but to launch a commando raid against civilian targets and kill such a large number of people in a small time.

I do believe that this has sent a signal to al-Qaeda senior leadership from Ahmed Abdi Godane. Whether or not he was the actual author of this operation, it sent a signal that al-Shabaab is an al-Qaeda affiliate that needs to be taken very seriously and that his leadership at this point is not in question, that they can launch these sorts of attacks.

And so preventing their affiliates, preventing their external operations group and the larger national insurgency movement that gives space for those extremists to operate, preventing them from continuing to hold such space in Somalia is really the critical element here. Something like the operation that is reported to have taken place in Barawe targeting a specific individual, al-Shabaab leader, or leader connected to al-Shabaab—that could do some temporary damage to the group, set back an immediate operational plan. But only by removing this group's safe havens and establishing a functioning national federal government that can actually address many of the clan tensions and undermine clan support and religious support for extremist splinter movements, that is going to be the only way to actually reduce the threat longer term.

Senator FLAKE. Well, thank you. My time is out. I appreciate it.

Senator COONS. Thank you, Senator Flake, for your engagement and your interest.

I have many more questions I would like to ask. Given the lateness of the hour, I may ask just one or two more briefly, if I might.

Dr. Le Sage, that last line of questioning suggests that we now face some time pressure to support an expansion of AMISOM, both its operational reach, its numeric strength, but that we are, at the same time, running against a clock to transition to a legitimate Somali security force because the longer security across the country is made possible by an external multinational force that is non-Somali, the more that creates the opportunity for recruitment and for al-Shabaab to simply cast this as an occupation army rather than a liberation force.

Would you agree with that? What do you think is the amount of time we actually have, and how pressing is this for regional security?

Dr. LE SAGE. Senator, given the length of time it is going to take to build up a professional and self-sustaining Somali national security force, including its army component, its intelligence component, and its policing component, it is urgent that we begin work on this today. At the same time, I think it is going to be urgent for the next several years, at least 5, to continue very significant support for the African Union mission in Somalia until the Somali national army forces actually come on line and can take over some of the static security positions that AMISOM currently holds.

If AMISOM was to leave today, the Somali Federal Government would very likely fall very quickly, and that is because the Somali National Army today is an amalgamation of different clan militias that used to report to warlords. And if you go in and look at the various brigades in Mogadishu that make up the Somali National Army today, it is pretty quick to identify which warlord and which militia faction they used to belong to. Their level of national loyalty, their interoperability between various subclans just in the city of Mogadishu is remarkably low.

And frankly, the Somali National Army that is being funded by the United States and European partners in Mogadishu is primarily crafted from one clan, the Hawiye clan, to the concern of all other clans in the regions across south-central Somalia, Puntland, and Somaliland. For this reason, we actually need very quickly to expand Somali National Army recruitment, take the clan militias from those other areas that either are a part of independent administrations or proxy forces for Ethiopia and Kenya and use salary payments, frankly, to integrate them into a national force, over time train them, equip them, and develop something professional. But that is going to take several years.

Senator COONS. Thank you.

If I might, Mr. Aynte, the issue of remittances, which you mentioned in passing, has been a real concern of mine. Describe, if you would, briefly the role of remittances from the United States and from Europe and how the Somali economy and the growing sort of capacity in Mogadishu and nationally would be affected if the mechanisms for transferring remittances were to be blocked? And what do you think we can and should do to try and sustain a pathway for legitimate, vetted remittances?

Mr. AYNTE. Senator, the scale of remittances to Somalia is larger than all international aid combined annually. It is about $1.5 billion a year coming from the Somali diaspora in the United States, Europe, Australia, and the Middle East and Africa. There are about 2 million Somalis scattered around the world sending money back to their relatives. So it is essentially the most important lifeline the Somali people have. I think the banks and other financial institutions have legitimate concerns about the rules and regulations both here in the United States but also in the United Kingdom where now Barclays Bank is blocking, or it is about to block, remittance companies to open bank accounts within Barclays. I think what the U.S. Government can do is to work with partners, particularly with the United Kingdom, to try and create a framework whereby the remittance companies can continue to send remittances legally to the Somali people.

The alternative now is, if Barclays goes ahead with its now promise to shut down on the Hawale companies in the U.K.—the alternative is that many people will go underground, and our ability to see the activities of money transfer from the West to Somalia will even become more constrained. So I think this is an urgent matter, one that has serious implications, both humanitarian, but as well as security both here for the United States but also for the Somali people.

Senator COONS. Thank you.

Dr. Hogendoorn, last question from me. The previous panel spoke some about the model of an African-led indirect action by the United States, financing an African-led multilateral force as being a possible role model for multilateral action for regional security. If we are at this sort of point of inflection where AMISOM either succeeds or fails and if actions like the attack in Nairobi put significant pressure on regional partners like Uganda, Kenya, Djibouti, Ethiopia, how vital is it for our interests on the continent and globally, how vital is it for Somalia's future that AMISOM succeed and that the regional partners continue to get bilateral support from the United States to stay engaged in this fight and to not withdraw?

Dr. HOGENDOORN. Well, as I mentioned in my testimony, I believe, as Dr. Andre Le Sage mentioned, that absent AMISOM, it is quite likely that the Somali National Government would collapse. And I think that AMISOM has done a remarkable job over the last 3 or 4 years to push al-Shabaab back at enormous cost in blood and treasure to the troop-contributing countries.

I think the largest challenge really, to some degree, is that while this has been a very effective military operation, the African Union at the moment still lacks the capacity to make this both an integrated political and military operation, which is why we have created this unwieldy hybrid between the United Nations, which has a political mandate, and the AU, which has a military mandate. And it has always been very, very difficult to try to meld those two organizations together since they have different cultures, they oftentimes have different leaders who sometimes do not get alone.

Currently the U.N. has transitioned to a new mission with a new special representative for the Secretary General. That mission was just established in June. So it is very early for us to be able to see how that will work. He does have instructions from the U.N. Security Council to cooperate with the AU. Those instructions are not very clear, as I mentioned in my testimony. And I think it remains a work in progress. And unfortunately, as I think all of my colleagues would agree, ultimately the solution in Somalia needs to be a political one and AMISOM needs to work within a political framework to achieve that goal, and kind of melding those two organizations and have them working toward the same goal has and will continue to be a challenge.

Senator COONS. Thank you.

Senator Flake, any further questions?

Senator FLAKE. Just one question.

Mr. Aynte, with regard to the diaspora, it is very involved, obviously, with $1.5 billion a year in terms of remittances. What is the feeling in the diaspora generally about the national government and the situation there? Can you give some sense of the feeling?

Mr. AYNTE. Well, you know, I used to be part of the diaspora myself, but now I am back home.

Senator FLAKE. I know it is not monolithic. I am not trying to suggest that, but give me some sense of——

Mr. AYNTE. Well, I think like most people in Somalia, the diaspora have welcomed the inauguration of this government in 2012 in huge numbers. I think a year into it, many people have realized that they probably had little higher expectations than realistic and are understandably disappointed with the low progress that has happened over the past year. But I think many Somalis continue to be optimistic and, more importantly, engaging what is going on in Somalia both not only in sending remittances but actually the diaspora do dominate the political structures across the country from Somaliland to Puntland to the federal government where as many as 50 percent of the entire Parliament is actually made up of diaspora. And something like 60 or 70 percent of the cabinet, any given cabinet, is diaspora. So the diaspora are vital to what is happening politically and socially and economically and what is going on and are engaged and sometimes are holding the government accountable to its national vision.

Senator FLAKE. Thank you.

Senator COONS. Thank you, Senator Flake.

Thank you to our witnesses today from the first and second panel. I will remind all of us where we began, which was the impact of the Government shutdown on the capacity of different agencies and departments within the United States to continue to carry out our development, our diplomacy, our intelligence, and our security missions. And I am grateful that all of our witnesses were able to come and testify today, and I would appreciate Senator Flake's cooperation in carrying forward this hearing, which I do think is an important part of our ongoing discussion about our role in Somalia and the region and the world.

I will keep the hearing record open until Friday of this week, October 11, so that members of the committee who were not able to join us today might submit written questions for the record.

And with that, this hearing is hereby adjourned.

[Whereupon, the hearing was adjourned.]